ENERGISED

ENERGISED

ENERGISED

ENERGISED

ENERGISED

ENERGISED
ENERGISED
ENERGISED
ENERGISED
ENERGISED

THE DAILY PRACTICE OF CONNECTED LEADERSHIP AND SUSTAINABLE WELLBEING

TIM JACK ADAMS

FOUNDER OF GREENX7

WILEY

First published 2025 by John Wiley & Sons Australia, Ltd

ISBN: 978-1-394-36007-9

A catalogue record for this book is available from the National Library of Australia

Registered Office
John Wiley & Sons Australia, Ltd. Level 4, 600 Bourke Street, Melbourne, VIC 3000, Australia

For details of our global editorial offices, customer services, and more information about Wiley products visit us at www.wiley.com.

Wiley also publishes its books in a variety of electronic formats and by print-on-demand. Some content that appears in standard print versions of this book may not be available in other formats.

Cover design by Wiley

Set in 11.5/15.5 pts and Utopia Std by Straive, Chennai, India.

CONTENTS

ABOUT THE AUTHOR

Tim Jack Adams is the founder of GreenX7, a science-backed wellbeing framework that helps individuals and organisations enhance energy, focus and resilience. Tim has spent over a decade guiding leaders and teams to reconnect with themselves and others through nature. Through corporate programs, retreats and coaching, he has worked with global organisations, including PwC, the Australian Defence Force, and Six Senses. A sought-after speaker, Tim's insights empower people to create lasting wellbeing habits, and sustainable success in work and life.

FOREWORDS

Neil Jacobs — CEO, Six Senses Hotels Resorts Spas

In a world where burnout and disconnection have become the norm, *Energised* offers a beacon of hope and a practical roadmap for reclaiming our vitality and purpose. As someone who embodies the principles of connected leadership, sustainable wellbeing and the transformative power of nature, my friend Tim Jack Adams has crafted a book that resonates deeply.

Through *Energised*, Tim generously shares wisdom gleaned from years of experience, guiding readers on a journey of self-discovery, meaningful connection and sustainable energy. This book is a testament to Tim's dedication to empowering others and fostering a more compassionate, resilient approach to leadership and life.

What sets *Energised* apart is its grounded, practical approach — eschewing fleeting trends for timeless, evidence-based strategies that yield tangible results. Whether you're a seasoned leader, entrepreneur or simply seeking a more balanced, fulfilling life, this book offers invaluable insights and tools to help you reconnect with your energy, purpose and the world around you.

I'm honoured to recommend *Energised* and excited for the positive impact it will have on readers. May its wisdom inspire you to live, lead and thrive in harmony with yourself, others and the natural world.

Josie Thomson — master coach, speaker, author and GreenX7 ambassador

I first met Tim Jack Adams at a transformative workshop while on retreat at Eden Health Retreat, Currumbin Valley, Queensland — a place where lives are recalibrated and souls are awakened. From the moment I stepped into that workshop with Tim, I knew I was embarking on a profound journey — one that would not only shift my perspective but also realign my entire way of living.

Tim's energy, wisdom and grounded approach were undeniable, and through his leadership, I discovered GreenX7, a way of life that promotes balance, health and harmony with nature. This was *gold*! I've been a nature freak all my life, and I loved Tim's approach from the get-go. Little did I know, however, that others were out there 'like me', and that this would be the beginning of a powerful connection that would shape my personal evolution and align me with a community of individuals committed to living in deeper connection with the Earth and themselves.

As I dove deeper into the GreenX7 philosophy, it became more than just a way of thinking — it also became a way of being. Every day, I carry the principles Tim has so passionately shared, living in alignment with the natural world, and constantly making choices that support not only my longevity but also my overall happiness and wellbeing. I am confident that you too will love this book and the practical strategies it offers you to improve your quality of life. Outlined through this book is a practice, a daily devotion to balance, wellness, and vitality that has enhanced every aspect of my life.

Becoming an ambassador for GreenX7 was not just a title. It's also a calling to inspire others to experience the life-changing power of living in tune with these principles. Through Tim's guidance, I've witnessed firsthand how the GreenX7 philosophy can uplift and transform, and now, with this book in your hands, you have the opportunity to experience that same shift.

Tim's words are more than just ideas — they are practical, grounded tools for a longer, healthier and happier life. This book will take you on a journey, just as it did for me, guiding you step by step toward a life lived in harmony with nature, supporting your physical health, and your emotional and spiritual wellbeing.

I encourage you to read with an open heart and a curious mind. The insights here have the power to transform how you view the world and your place within it. Tim's passion and authenticity shine through every page, and I am confident that his wisdom will support you on your own journey to thriving — just as it continues to support me every day.

Here's to living in harmony with nature, to a deeper connection with yourself and others, and to the long, healthy, joyful life that awaits you.

INTRODUCTION

Our magnificent bodies and minds have evolved over centuries to explore, create, challenge, love and inspire — to be participators in life. We're not meant to be cooped up, hunched over and staring into a light box for hours, days, weeks, years or over our whole lifetime. We're not meant to be spectators.

I worry about a world that focuses less on connecting through conversation and heartfelt moments, and more on connecting through a device. I see too many people together, but not connected. The kid watching on, while both parents sit on their phones at breakfast. The friends at high tea who seem to care more about the perfect shot to represent their perfect lives — which only exist on social media. The dad who watches sport on the television, while his son throws a ball against the wall outside. The work team who eat lunch at their desk liking photos of people they've never met, rather than talk to each other and connect outside for an hour. This is the world I too often find myself in. A world where my smile is a distraction that takes people away from a world of being a spectator. Yes, technology has evolved in leaps and bounds these past decades. But can we say the same for our minds, bodies and souls? Or are we getting too used to playing someone else's games?

I believe we have everything we need within us and our natural environment to look after our mental, emotional and physical health. In a world that too often turns to technology to try to solve its problems, I want to inspire people to turn to each other. To achieve this, we need to reconnect to ourselves, each other and the natural environment.

Losing our 'true north'

Society as a collective seems to have lost its way. We no longer seem to know where to find our 'true north' — and, in many cases, don't even know how to read the compass.

Many experts have argued that, for the first time in human history, today's children could live a shorter lifespan than their parents due to poor nutritional choices and living a sedentary lifestyle — and spend more of their years living with chronic disease.[1] As well as these health concerns, being plugged into technology through devices 24/7 is also having a detrimental effect on our mental health.

According to the Australian Government's Productivity Commission in 2020, mental illness, including conditions such as anxiety and depression, was estimated to cost the nation nearly $220 billion annually, factoring in healthcare expenses, lost productivity, and related costs. The financial burden of a sedentary lifestyle is also significant, with Australian Government estimates from 2018 indicating an economic cost of approximately A$11.8 billion annually. (With predictions this could blow out to A$87.7 billion by 2032 if nothing is done.)[2]

Can you imagine if we could put that money towards education, helping the homeless and improving our lifestyles?

Our lifestyles are a major contributor to our health, wellbeing and longevity. Only around 20 to 30 per cent of who, what and how we are can be blamed on our genetics — when it comes to our longevity, the rest is up to us, and making sure we're dealing ourselves the right cards.[3]

So far, however, the deck we are working with isn't looking hopeful:

- *Childhood obesity projections:* By 2050, researchers project that half of Australian children will be overweight or obese, highlighting significant societal challenges.[4]

- *Mental health among youth:* In 2023, approximately 46 per cent of young Australian females and 32 per cent of young males aged 16 to 24 have experienced a mental health disorder in the past year, indicating a growing mental health crisis.[5]

- *Chronic health conditions:* According to 2022 data, over 81 per cent of Australians have at least one long-term health condition, with nearly 50 per cent living with a chronic condition, underscoring widespread health challenges.[6]

- *Suicide rates:* Suicide remains a leading cause of death among Australians aged 15 to 44, with at least six Australians dying from suicide daily and an additional 30 attempting it.[7]

The key to reversing these statistics lies in some simple yet often overlooked activities — play, movement and genuine connection. We tend to search for complex solutions, but the truth is much of what we need as a society — and as leaders — to restore our wellbeing and that of our teams can be found in the joy of moving our bodies, immersing ourselves in nature, and engaging meaningfully with others.

Somewhere along the way, many of us have lost touch with the things that keep us grounded. We traded outdoor adventures for screen time, swapped real conversations for digital interactions, and sacrificed movement for convenience. We became more disconnected — from ourselves, from nature, and from each other.

But here's the good news — we can change this. We don't need to reinvent the wheel; we just need to realign with what already exists within us. Everything you read in this book has been experienced by thousands of people all over the world, from many walks of life and in many industries — so it's safe to say it works. I'm living proof, and so are others you will hear from in the following chapters.

When I look back over the years at the work that I've done for myself and others to thrive sustainably through our GreenX7 workshops and keynotes, plus the 1000s of hours consumed by research, four key attributes stand out: the ability to be grounded, resilient, open and well — that is, the ability to GROW. And this ability starts with your personal battery.

How's your battery?

Every day most of us make a deliberate decision to plug in our devices. From our phones and laptops to even our smart watches, we make sure to recharge their batteries. And yet, how often are we doing the same for ourselves?

How often do you make the deliberate choice to recharge your own battery so that you can wake up every day and be as healthy, happy and productive as possible? And how often are you checking in on your team's battery?

When our personal batteries are low, we often make similar choices as when our device batteries are low. If my phone battery is low, for example, I close as many applications as possible. In the same way, in the past if my personal battery was low, I would close out people around me. When my phone's battery gets even lower, I dim the light on it. Once again, in the past, I was doing the same to myself. When my battery was low, so was my internal light. I no longer shined as brightly, and I became only a dimmed-down version of my best self.

What I realised was that, just like my devices, I needed to reconnect and recharge every day so my personal battery didn't go flat. Instead of simply surviving or functioning, I could charge my battery up every day — and I could thrive.

Focusing on your battery means focusing on your own wellness — and that means making a deliberate effort to look after your mental, emotional, physical and spiritual self. The first step is understanding the areas that make up your battery, and I cover these in part II. The next step is recharging your battery, and I outline the tools to do so in part III. I then pull all these aspects together in part IV. In each of the chapters, I've also included lots of practical tips, action points, and ways to set your intention. You're about to dive into a practical, how-to guide to thriving sustainably.

Before we get started, a quick note on some of the terms I use through this book to avoid any confusion. (Just in case you're anything like me when I got started on this journey — I used to think looking after your 'wellbeing' meant going to a day spa!) Here's how I now define some important terms:

- *Wellbeing:* Being well, mentally, emotionally, physically and spiritually.

- *Wellness:* The deliberate effort to be in a state of wellbeing.

- *Your battery:* The many parts that make up wellbeing.

So, buckle up! We're about to launch into how we got here in the first place and, more importantly, how we can turn things around. And don't worry—plenty of fun is waiting for you at the finish line!

PART I

SETTING THE SCENE

From the moment you were born, the first sentence in your novel was written. Each day a new page has turned and each year a new chapter has closed. You don't know how many chapters are left in this novel of yours, but you can control and predict one thing: whether this novel of yours is a page-turner — one that you can't put down, filled with love, life and adventures, where the main character tells their own hero's journey — or a book that your family and children allow to sit in a dusty box hidden away, because the only story you had to tell was that of others.

It's time for you to disconnect from a life filled with the expectations of others, dig deep into your heart and soul and understand what it is that makes your heart sing. It's time to live a life that's true to yourself — not one that is being pushed towards you.

It's time for you to reconnect with yourself and understand who you are and what it is you want from this life. It's time for you to reconnect with others and create the warmth of relationships we know give our lives great satisfaction. It's time for you to reconnect to the great outdoors — the source of our fondest memories and the space where others come into our lives through meaningful connections.

Your time is now! You can grow into the best version of you and start living your best life — a life that will be one hell of a page-turner! And the greatest gift of all, you have the opportunity to inspire others along the way.

Throughout the first chapter of part I, I run through my own evolution as I worked out what made up my battery and how I could recharge it for everyday wellness. In chapter 2, I then run through the main reasons your battery can get so low — and provide an overview of what you can do about it.

Before we begin, remember this: no matter where you are or how you feel right now—it's enough. However, I also want you to think about the possibility of what your life could be if, day by day, you implement the positive steps that I present in this book.

Take a moment now to think about the best version of you. What does it look like—who are you with, what are you doing and, most importantly, how does it feel? Picturing where you want to go can help you understand why you want to go there, and reflecting with compassion can show that the choices you have previously made (the ways you have coped in the past) may not be serving you well anymore. So, close your eyes and visualise who, where and what you want to be, so together we can take you there.

Chapter 1

My evolution — and that of GreenX7

I grew up like so many other Australian males — taught to hide my emotions to avoid being bullied or seen as weak among my peers and male role models. After a while of living like this, you forget about feelings and emotions, and that you have a heart that is capable of caring. You become great at communicating but forget how to connect. You care about those you love — and you want to care about yourself — but don't really know how.

This vicious cycle goes on and on, from father to son — a process on repeat. Each generation wants to change, to break the cycle, but just doesn't understand how. Often, the only thing that breaks this cycle is some sort of catalyst or event that has such a significant impact on your life that you can no longer ignore it.

That's what happened to me — after 20 years of living behind a mask, the time came to take it off.

And so we get to my story, which is just like the stories of so many around me. The events may not seem significant, but that's the problem — they are too significant to stay hidden. Just like my emotions that bubbled to the surface, what I've created for myself to thrive sustainably needs to be shared.

In this chapter, I share the significant events that, when I look back, I realised have contributed to my thoughts and actions, and shaped who I am today. While this book is a guide to help you grow rather than an autobiography, I first want to create a connection with you. Sharing where I came from can help you understand how I got to writing this book in the first place.

Growing up in the 'Brady Bunch'

I was born on the Gold Coast, Australia, in 1982 to Gary and Samantha, two years after my older brother, Sam. Mum says I was a happy kid, always smiling and laughing, and some of my earliest memories are of the beaches at Currumbin and Coolangatta. I had curly blond hair, big blue eyes and an ever-present mischievous smile.

When Mum remarried, my little brother, Nick, was born, five years my junior. Growing up, the three of us brothers were mad keen on basketball, letting our imaginations run wild pretending we were NBA All-Stars. I was Magic Johnson, Sam was Michael Jordan and Nick was Larry Johnson. At the age of 12 (yes, it was the '90s), I got a job in a trading cards shop Trading Faces in the Oasis Shopping Centre, Broadbeach. I'd catch the bus up and get paid $5 an hour plus another $5 for lunch. I thought I was the luckiest kid in the world.

A big part of my childhood was moving. Mum loved to renovate houses and by the time I moved out at 17 we had lived in

18 different places — so we had all became very good at packing and unpacking. The other constant in our childhood was music, with our household always filled with the beats of Michael Jackson or Black Box and neighbourhood kids dancing in the lounge room.

By the time high school came around for me, our family of three boys suddenly turned into a family of six boys when Mum married Don (nicknamed 'Chief'). We became somewhat of the 'Brady Bunch' with three boys on Mum's side, and three boys on Don's. Together we lived in a little three-bedroom fibro beach shack squeezed between all the oceanfront mansions in Palm Beach on the Gold Coast. Even though the house was tight and chaotic, with all the brothers trying to work out the pecking order, we had the Pacific Ocean as our backyard — which ignited my love of surfing. I remember many days setting off on my push bike to school along the beach bike paths — and then turning back around for my second surf session of the morning. Nature always seemed to have more persuasion over me than academics.

Our little beach shack had an open-door policy, with at least 10 boys around most days, creating chaos. If there wasn't any surf, it was a playing field of testosterone, where shenanigans were an everyday part of life. I was second last in the pecking order and compared to Don's boys I was very meek and shy, wanting to fit in but not quite having the grunt, confidence and stature to play rough.

When we all started living together, being picked on was a daily occurrence, and I remember one day going to Mum and asking her for advice on how to make them stop. At the time, Mum's advice was exactly what I needed to hear: 'Don't let them see you cry'. So I didn't — and I took that advice so literally that I didn't cry for another 13 years. To fit in and be 'one of the boys',

I started to hide my soft exterior and push down my emotions. Over those teenage years, I learned how to adapt and overcome, as so many other Aussie boys do. I learned to be sarcastic, act tough and use my fists, and was always trying to do things that made me look cool in front of my mates.

By the time I was 15, the little boy who smiled and laughed was now a teenager with attitude. Growing up in such a male-dominated household, where physical strength and courage was prized over emotions and academics, it wasn't long before school just became a place to hang out with mates — unless the surf was good.

These high school years really shaped who I was to become over the next 15 years of my life, and how I would treat myself and others around me.

Becoming a sponge for information

By the time I had scraped through to my last year of high school, I had no idea what I wanted to be or what I was going to do with myself. The only thing I was vaguely interested in was becoming an apprentice mechanic with my best mate, Mitch. I went to my school guidance counsellor to ask for a letter of recommendation to join Mitch as an apprentice mechanic — and instead was told I wasn't smart enough. After that, I didn't see much point in trying too hard at school.

My mindset was extremely narrow back then, with a feeling of almost zero opportunities ahead of me. I didn't understand that you could grow and become or do anything you wanted to — that was, until I listened to my first Anthony Robbins cassette tape. I even remember where I was, living in my uncle's downstairs basement with its whitewashed concrete walls, listening on my blue Sanyo Walkman. I got completely swept up by Robbins's enthusiasm and passion for life, and his argument that if you put your mind to it, you can achieve anything!

For my 18th birthday, instead of mag wheels for my VL Holden Commodore, I asked for the complete cassette series of Anthony Robbins. I also read *Rich Dad Poor Dad* (by Robert T. Kiyosaki and Sharon Lechter, published in 1997), and so many other self-help books on my journey to better myself. I became an absolute sponge for information, wanting to read everything I could about business, property and how to become an entrepreneur. I started a clothing company for the surf and skate industry and worked for one of my best mates, Dave Prince, in his sporting store, trying to learn as much as I could.

I was so obsessed with generating wealth that I stopped doing all the things that I loved, including surfing. By the age of 20, I was burned out, depressed and jaded. I had forgotten what made my heart sing and was living within the expectations of society. One day my Mum came across my journal when she was visiting, and read how her once happy-go-lucky kid was becoming depressed and jaded with life. The conversation that ensued led me in a whole new direction.

Shortly after that conversation with Mum, I'd packed up all my possessions and was on a plane to London, ready for the well-worn route of the Australian backpacker. I lived briefly in both London and Laggan, a little village in Scotland. I also spent time in many places throughout western Europe and even got to spend a few nights in the Sahara Desert, getting caught in a sandstorm in my sleeping bag. I continued to travel abroad through Asia, and when I finally arrived back in Oz, I packed up my HJ60 LandCruiser with all my worldly possessions (none) to explore both Australia and myself some more, before growing roots in a place I would finally call home.

During my travels, I kept a journal, and on the back page I drew a line going straight down the middle. On one side I listed 'likes' and on the other 'dislikes'. During those years of travel, I was very deliberate in trying many different aspects of life – from different landscapes to different types of work, and even varying types of girlfriends. I guess deep down I wanted to understand what and who it was that made me happy. Or maybe I was just trying to work out who I was, and what and where I wanted to be.

I lived in cities, jungles, coastal towns, the outback, on reefs and mountains. I built log cabins in Scotland, worked as a barman, a labourer, a stockman in Deniliquin, at a rice mill, as a salesman, and a divemaster. And, throughout this time, I kept jotting down my likes and dislikes, until finally, in 2009 at the age of 27, I created my dream job.

Starting my first business — and growing slowly

Using my list of likes and dislikes, the 'dream job' I created was my own business — Watersports Guru, an eco-tourism business on the Tweed coast, offering snorkelling with the turtles, paddle boarding and kayaking. The business combined all my loves and everything I had learned over the many years of my travels and experiences. By that stage, I realised I was a terrible employee, so the only sensible move was to work for myself!

I knew exactly what I needed to do to create a job I would be passionate about. Over the years, it had become very clear to me that I needed to work in nature, especially on the water. Also, I inherited the gift of the gab from my parents, who are both very charismatic — and storytelling plays a wonderful role when introducing people to experiences.

I tendered for a license to operate Watersports Guru on the beautiful nine-kilometre stretch of Cudgen Creek nature reserve, which runs through the heart of Kingscliff in northern New South Wales. I also teamed up with a skipper named Mal, a short, stocky, tanned bloke with a big voice and even bigger persona, who I used to be a deckhand for while I was an apprentice divemaster. Together, we created the 'Snorkel with the Turtles' tour at Cook Island, just off the coast from us at Fingal Heads.

In those early days, my business consisted of owning 12 masks and snorkels, 8 kayaks and a website. I had created something from scratch with my own money and was determined for it to grow into a prosperous business. It was, however, a very slow start, as back then the Tweed, and especially Kingscliff, was not known as a tourist destination. I fostered friendships with the general managers of the local Mantra and Peppers hotel groups, which gave me the opportunity to establish an activities desk in the foyer of each hotel. Little did I know it at the time, but when I walked in each morning, I'd be saying hello to my future wife, Carly.

Every morning, I would sit at one of my desks, booking in guests for either our snorkelling or kayaking tours. Then, I would race over to the Fingal boathouse and be the guide for our snorkel trips, have a BBQ lunch with skipper, Mal, and the guests, and then race back to our Salt boathouse to run a kayak tour. My trusty Land Rover Defender could be seen whizzing back and forth all day long with guests on board to experience our activities. They were long, exciting days — and I absolutely loved it!

This was all just after the 2008 global financial crisis. Through this time, I had watched many of my scuba diving clients lose not only their fortunes but also their families. One of my then mentors, Gary, said something that really stuck with me: 'Always live well within your means'. I didn't understand the full impact of that statement at the time but it has been a guiding principle of mine ever since, and one that remains a core foundation of my wellbeing.

With Gary's advice guiding me, along with a lot of hard work, year on year, Guru grew to offer paddle boarding, kids adventure programs and whale watching. I even started Teambuilding Guru to cater for the corporations that were conferencing at the hotels. I now had over 12 staff in the peak season, and one of those staff was about to change who I was at a fundamental level.

Active engagement in nature

By 2012, Guru was coming along swimmingly. We'd even converted an old 1960s BP service station in the heart of Kingscliff to an activities hub, where you could hire everything from bikes and surfboards to fishing rods. We tried to offer anything that would get people — and especially kids — outdoors and having fun.

Around the same time, while sitting down at the creek hiring out our water sport equipment and watching people play and connect to nature, I found I was repeatedly asking myself, 'Why is it when we actively engage in nature, we seem to be healthier and happier?'

I had spent the last 10 years of my life in the adventure, education and ecotourism industries, and had watched not only my own mood and health improve in nature, but also that of those around me. I looked at my peers in tourism and compared them to those of my friends who lived in cities or worked 9 to 5 under UV lights. I knew innately that each time I went snorkelling or jumped on a paddle board, playing in nature, I felt happier. I was sure a link existed between active engagement in nature and feeling better.

I dived into all the research I could find in this field, and came across Dr Jules Pretty, a professor at the University of Sussex who was one of the pioneers behind the term 'green exercise' — that is, physical exercise undertaken in natural environments. I devoured everything I could find written by Pretty, highlighted every second paragraph and continued to delve deeper into the world of green exercise. My obsession had begun.

Over the next few years, I read a library of research, talked to academics, practitioners and neuroscientists, and started to formulate the framework I now call the GreenX7 tools for everyday wellness.

Around the same time, I hired an operations manager for Guru, an outdoor educator named Bri, who could instantly make someone feel valued — a gift that I believe is one of the greatest a human can possess. Over the years, Bri helped me open myself up and put heart into what we were doing, through creating a deeper connection beyond communication.

When I looked back at my teenage years, and all through my twenties, I realised I had become adept at being a great communicator but had zero capacity to connect at a deeper level. I was always willing to have deep discussions intellectually but talking about matters of the heart definitely wasn't my strong point. I had some amazing relationships over the years, but all would eventually end. Back then I never understood why, but it was becoming blatantly obvious to me that I had a very limited emotional IQ.

Like so many blokes, I had become great at the 'masculine' — able to fit into any situation by drinking beer, talking sports and generally peacocking around to make sure I was showing other men I could handle myself. I spent 15 years building a perfect mask of masculinity, only to realise that it was damaging the one thing I really wanted — connection.

My book of dreams

And so began a whole new chapter in my life, and one that would lead me to writing this book. I was on a journey of wellness. I delved deeper into green exercise, and continued to connect with like-minded individuals all over the world who were engaging in nature-based research, collecting more and more data.

I also became fascinated with people watching. I would sit and watch people at cafes, parks, beaches and shopping centres, catching all their little interactions. I studied how people lived their lives, and whether the research I'd read was able to be practically implemented into daily life. I filled journals — or, as I called each one, my 'book of dreams' — with notes, diagrams and learnings, trying to work out what would stick or what would fall away when it came to developing routines and habits.

I also looked deeper into my own life and started to run all sorts of scenarios on a daily, weekly and monthly basis to make sure what I was creating worked. I tracked what made me energetic, moody, content, grounded, resilient, open, healthy and, most of all, well.

All my observations, practical implementations, research and data eventually all came together into a beautiful framework that everyone could use to create positive change. This framework consisted of the seven tools I outline in part III: movement, environment, earthing, time, connection, breath, reflection. When combined into an activity or experience, these tools created a recipe for everyday wellness — and the beauty of this framework was that you could tailor it to almost anyone, anywhere, for their lifestyle. GreenX7 was born — I had cracked the code for everyday wellness … almost.

Truly understanding the importance of value, meaning and belonging

Over the next couple of years, I continued to evaluate the program — gathering data, continuing my research and observing the GreenX7 tools in action. I started to formulate how my team and I were going to deliver them to those who needed them — and, from the data we were uncovering, it was a large portion of the population.

I also delved further into the gap between just communicating and really connecting with someone. One of the GreenX7 tools is connection, and I was beginning to realise that this is the foundation of all wellness. With connection, we plant the seed to foster self-worth, and self-worth is a vital component of looking after ourselves. I realised connection could be broken down into three 'touchpoints' that, if focused on each day, would help create self-worth in yourself and those around you. Those three touchpoints are value, meaning and belonging.

As these realisations were coming to me, and I was beginning to take my own mask off, the course of my life completely changed. It was 2015, and by this stage I had been running the Snorkel with the Turtles tours for over six years with my mate and business partner, Mal, who would skipper the boat, and put on a BBQ when we got back to the Fingal boathouse.

Our days went by like this...

Meet and greet guests at the Fingal boathouse at 9 am, gear them up in wetsuits, masks and snorkels, and provide a briefing about snorkelling and an educational talk about the marine life we would likely encounter. We'd then depart from the jetty and take the 15-minute boat trip past Fingal Head, one of the most beautiful beaches in Australia, hang out with the local pod of inshore bottlenose dolphins for a few minutes and then make our way to Cook Island. For the next two hours we would be in heaven, snorkelling around on the reefs, and just being amazed at the life that the rocky outcrop attracts.

Cook Island is one of those rare places — only a 15-minute boat ride off the Tweed coast, and you can be hanging out with green, loggerhead and hawksbill turtles, from juveniles to elders the size of coffee tables. You can also see a plethora of other subtropical marine life, including the occasional manta ray and humpback whales in winter. It is my home away from home, and where my life motto of 'be the turtle' originated as, over the many years of hanging out with turtles, I realised they have a sense of calmness, a kind of 'go with the flow' attitude. They never fight their surroundings or the currents but instead wait for the right moment and then flow with ease.

I first started diving this island when I was a trainee divemaster with Kirra Dive at the age of 21, freshly returned from travelling overseas with a head full of dreadlocks. I would work as a deckhand, accumulating hours for my coxswain ticket, with Mal as the skipper grabbing the anchor ropes, serving up hot soup on our surface intervals and showing me how to cross the treacherous Tweed bar.

Over those years, Mal had become a great mentor and mate, and I'd loved watching his two kids, Max and Indie, practically grow up in the water. They reminded me of Steve Irwin's kids, always up for any adventure and stuck like glue to their dad. Mal always seemed to be the happiest bloke I knew, and people were drawn to his infectious love for life and an easy laugh.

To me, we were living our best lives. I still remember sitting on the boathouse deck overlooking the Tweed River with a Tooheys New in hand, watching the sunsets, talking about how we were going to make our tours even better and what else could we do together to share our beautiful backyard with others. Like most blokes, we'd just chew the fat over a couple of beers before it was time to head back home.

That's how our days went — until one morning I received a phone call as I was gearing up to head to the boat. Chris, a mutual skipper friend of ours was ringing to let me know Mal had been found dead in his boathouse, the same place I had left him a day prior. He had died by suicide.

After 12 years of working, playing and running the snorkel tours together, Mal was gone. Even now, many years on I still feel a range of emotions when I bring up that memory. I feel it in the pit of my stomach — grief, sadness, anger. To this day, I still have no idea why; all I know is that it hurts like hell. His two kids, Max and Indi, who loved their dad immensely, had lost their hero.

Suicide sucks.

And then begins all those questions that float around your head. What wasn't said? What did Mal tell me that I didn't hear, which could potentially have saved his life? What did he keep bottled up inside that would one day be the catalyst for his suicide? How could I have not seen it coming? Could I have done something to prevent it?

I will never know the answers to these questions, but I know one thing for sure — we need to change this culture of men feeling like they can't have the conversation that could save their lives. Beneath our rough, tough exteriors lies the heart of a boy who still craves love, reassurance and connection. Somewhere along the way, most of us are taught that speaking about our feelings isn't 'manly'. So we bottle them up, bury them deep, and convince ourselves that silence is strength. Picking up the phone to call a mate and talk about the hard stuff feels like an impossible task — like breaking some unspoken code. But the truth is real courage isn't in the pretending; it's in the willingness to be seen, to be heard, and to be honest about what's really going on inside. Our country is built on the attitudes of 'she'll be right mate' and 'harden up son'. Unfortunately, that attitude is responsible for suicide being the leading cause of death for men aged 15 to 44 years, and for over three-quarters of all people who die by suicide being male.[8]

After Mal took his life, I constantly asked myself, 'How could I have prevented that?' and 'What didn't I hear or see that Mal was trying to tell me?' I started looking at ways that I could get blokes to 'open up' without putting up a wall or throwing on their tough exteriors. I needed to find a way to create deeper conversations.

Finding a rhythm for everyday wellness

Around this same time, things were also starting to take shape at GreenX7. We not only had created a framework based around the seven tools that could be used to create a rhythm for everyday wellness, but were also looking at the broader picture of being able to measure wellbeing and resilience. Over the past three years, we had gathered some brilliant minds, both within Australia and overseas, who would eventually become our 'brains board'. We were still gathering and garnishing loads of research and data, and continually refining our framework to deliver our message to anyone who would listen.

A great opportunity came up in 2016 when we were asked to deliver the GreenX7 program to the guests of Eden Health Retreat, in the Gold Coast hinterland, on a weekly basis. These guests were the perfect audience, visiting the retreat to either rebuild from burning out or just recharge, before going back into their busy lives.

Over that year we trialled and assessed everything that we had learned over those last three years to create a succinct workshop — one we were very proud of and hoped would have ever-lasting results.

We knew wellness was the deliberate effort to look after yourself in four ways: mentally, emotionally, physically and spiritually. Now, all we had to do was identify the aspects — or as we called them 'areas' — that made up wellbeing, and how we could practically measure and improve them. These areas would form the elements of our battery. (I say, 'all we had to do', but the eight areas were hotly contested among our team, the brains board, our academics on the GreenX7 research and development project, friends, family and gosh knows who else.)

Eventually, we came up with our eight wellness areas that form the basis of our battery — and the foundation of wellbeing. And, yes, we also created a way to measure these areas so we could have a benchmark to understand if people were merely surviving, functioning or in fact thriving. I introduce these wellness areas and the benchmarks in chapter 2, and expand on each of the areas in the chapters in part II.

Working on the sustainability of wellness

From 2016 onwards, word started to spread about GreenX7 and we started facilitating our 'everyday wellness' workshops across Australia in all different industries — from education, corporate and tourism to even with some of Australia's top athletes. We hosted a three-day workshop at United World College (UWC) in China and were invited to Singapore on behalf of EarthCheck, to look at integrating GreenX7 into the hospitality industry for both staff and guest experiences. I was also invited to keynote speak at events and conferences, which luckily my team-building days had prepared me for — and I found that I loved it! I had to pinch myself everyday — how did a kid from the Gold Coast who barely graduated high school and wanted to become a car mechanic end up delivering wellness all over the world?

Over the next two years, the team and I worked hard to keep improving GreenX7 and make sure we had created an extremely simple and effective framework to improve wellbeing for not only individuals but also teams and organisations.

As part of this, we created the Sustainability of Wellness (SOW) model, which enables us to unpack somebody's life — measuring both their willingness and ability to look after themselves — and then rebuild it, curating their purpose, and finding value, meaning and belonging in their everyday life to help them create the self-worth they need to want to look after themselves.

Researching alternative health frameworks led me to the UK's Green Social Prescribing initiative, where doctors prescribe nature-based activities instead of traditional medication, and have seen improvements in patients' wellbeing and life satisfaction (see chapter 2 for more on this). This led me to look at how green prescriptions within Australia could help with our sports and tourism industry.

We also were invited to join Impact Academy, a social enterprise incubator that helps growing start-ups create positive changes on a larger scale, and this prompted us to reconsider the best method of delivering our message.

Disconnect to reconnect

We had come to a crossroads — to somewhat of a moral dilemma. From our research, we knew that people were already spending an average of 46 hours on screens each week[9], with teenagers only slightly behind at 43.6 hours per week.[10] Our framework was created to inspire people to disconnect from screens and reconnect to themselves and others through nature. So our dilemma was this: do we stay small and only ever facilitate face-to-face workshops, or do we advance, using technology to scale and reach all four corners of the globe using an app-based platform?

After much deliberation, we decided that we needed to reach people where they were and try to inspire them to 'disconnect to reconnect'. At the same time, we would continue our workshops and retreats, because we loved being facilitators and coaches, and could see the benefits these programs were having. Getting people in a natural setting was where the magic happened. Triggering the natural production of oxytocin and feeling the sun on your face and grass between your toes is a catalyst to getting out of your head and into your heart. It was why we didn't go to a corporate head office to deliver our program, but found a space that would allow people to disconnect from work and reconnect to themselves and others.

Once we started developing the app, however, we realised how advantageous it was going to be in the following ways:

- By asking eight simple questions — related to the eight wellness areas of our battery charge — we had the ability to calculate 'battery percentage'. This created a benchmark and a way to measure wellbeing, in turn creating an easy way to communicate with others — through simply asking, 'How's your battery'?

- We could use the data to produce a wellness report for each individual, and highlight areas that needed improvement.

- We could use an algorithm to calculate what GreenX7 tools would be most powerful in recharging a person's battery.

- Based on the GreenX7 tools identified, we could then look at what activities best supported these tools.

Essentially, we had created a world's first through being able to tailor suggested activities based on a person's wellbeing in 60 seconds — it was brilliant!

But, for me, we achieved something far more important — something that I had been trying to crack since Mal passed. This was the ability to check in on your mates, and not just at a rudimentary level. We had created a tool that, in just 60 seconds, allows anyone — a family member, friend, colleague, patient or coach — to share their wellness report via the app. Instantly, the recipient receives a notification with a clear snapshot of the sender's wellbeing and tailored recommendations on how to recharge. We had essentially taken the guess work out of wellbeing. We called it 'Connect. Share. Care.'

An international luxury wellness hotel group saw the app's potential for its staff and guests, and committed to using the program once it was up and running. We worked out a way to incorporate location-based activities within the wellness report, so staff and guests were suggested tailored activities in their immediate vicinity, based on their personal battery needs. This also enabled us to develop a comprehensive dashboard, allowing us to aggregate and analyse wellness data on a larger scale. By collecting real-time insights from users, we could identify patterns, trends and key areas where individuals were struggling or thriving. This data-driven approach not only provided a clearer understanding of people's needs but also allowed for more personalised support, targeted interventions and informed decision making. The dashboard became a powerful tool for tracking overall wellbeing, measuring progress, and implementing proactive strategies to enhance health and performance — and it could be used for individuals, or across teams and organisations.

I now use the app during my keynote speeches and workshops. As I talk, the group scans a QR code that takes them to a site where they enter responses across the eight wellness areas. Their collective battery is then calculated, which allows me to see exactly what wellness areas I need to focus on and what activities to undertake that day to help them recharge.

By now we had created our GreenX7 board of advisors, all of whom I was extremely proud to have on our team. They are people with sharp minds and big hearts and doing wonderful things in their individual fields. I'm a big believer in the value of having mentors in your life, and of asking for help when you need it. My team and I couldn't do what we do without the incredible support of this group of brilliant hearts and minds — each one deeply committed to a shared vision of improving lives and making a meaningful impact on humanity. Their expertise, passion and belief in our mission fuel our work, helping us drive real change where it matters most.

Finding a new purpose

Then came 2020, and the world as we all know it changed forever. The COVID pandemic reached across the world and, like so many of us, my whole professional existence ceased to exist overnight. One minute I felt like I was riding a wave of success in my career, and the next I felt as though I had been wiped out. Our overseas contracts were put on hold and even back home in Australia, 94 per cent of our conferences and events were cancelled. I remember saying to Carly, now my wife, that I didn't have a purpose anymore. She replied, 'Yes you do, babe. It's just nobody wants it'. I didn't know whether to laugh or cry.

Then, on 2 December 2020, our little boy, Sonny, was born — and became the silver lining to my troubled times. I was now a doting father and, most importantly, I had a new purpose: to be the very best dad I could possibly be. Two years later, Carly gave birth to our very cute but mischievous daughter, Frankie. From the moment she was born on the lounge room floor (not planned) she has been a handful. (As we always say, lucky she's cute!)

Having that down time through COVID allowed me to reset to what is truly important and, like it did for many of us, gave me the opportunity to stop, reflect and live from my own expectations. We created a new rhythm for our family, based around Carly's work roster as a firefighter of four days on four days off, that would allow us plenty of time to connect and have lots of family adventures. We also created little mini traditions that the kids now look forward to each week, such as 'Friday family fun day' and 'pancake Sunday'. Our family motto is always have fun and be kind, and I feel we are doing a pretty good job of it.

I'm often coaching parents who are also leaders in very demanding roles. They work so hard to give their children the very best but sometimes forget that their 'very best' needs to include their time. Now as a dad, I must adhere to my own advice.

This book is a guidebook to thrive sustainably, through creating the ability and willingness to want to look after yourself, and learning the tools and knowledge to do so. And, most importantly, it's a guidebook for not just creating time for happiness, but also being happy, healthy and proud of who you're becoming.

It's about reconnecting to yourself, each other and the natural environment that surrounds us all because you want to achieve everyday wellness — you want to make the deliberate effort to constantly seek out the best version of you.

I started writing this book in 2017 but kept putting it away, never quite having the secret sauce to finish it. When Sonny came along, I knew it was the right time to pick it back up again and finish it. Frankie's birth only made the feeling stronger. I wanted to create a guidebook I could hand down to my kids to hopefully prevent them from wasting their younger years, believing they had to be someone or something that they're not. In other words, I wanted to give them the head start in life I wish I had.

My journey to strive to be the best version of myself is never-ending, because I'm not sure any of us know exactly what the best version of ourselves really looks like. I guess, though, if I look back to where I was 10 years ago, I am extremely proud of the man I have become.

Here are some things that I am most proud of so far in my life:

- I now enjoy my brain. I know that may seem a strange thing to say, but I like being me — I enjoy my thoughts and I have good things to say about myself. I stopped drinking alcohol some years ago now because I didn't need to escape anymore. I was content just being in my head and found other ways to dissolve my anger or frustrations.

- I now have the ability and willingness to help others. The ability comes through my energy and vitality to serve my purpose, and my willingness is my why. Before I just did; now I know why.

- I have the most amazing wife and mother to our two children. Carly reflects the work I have put into myself in being the very best I can be and the person I continue to strive to be. Without doing the work, I would never have attracted someone so special.

- I'm a proud, loving and devoted father to my boy, Sonny, and daughter, Frankie. I have devoted as much effort to being an amazing dad as I have with my pursuit of wellness, because I believe it's my highest calling.

Of course, as well as being for my children, this book is also for you. No matter what age or point along your journey you are, you can always find time to heal, learn, grow, and share what you know — even if that's just a little more than the person you're trying to help. I hope you will take the learnings you discover in the following chapters and share them with your family and friends — and with your work colleagues and those you lead. Recognise that giving our best to the people we love and to our selves includes giving our time. Like any skill you wish to acquire, it's about devoting your time and effort into something you are passionate about — and I hope you find your passion here.

Chapter 2

Finding a new way to reconnect and recharge

Before I jump into the detail of the main elements in your battery, and the tools to recharge them, let's take a moment to understand why we are doing the work in the first place. Anyone who wants to create change — be it a person, team, community or any other entity — first needs to be in enough pain, or dis-ease, that they are willing to put the effort into creating a new habit to move forward and away from that pain — otherwise, the change just won't stick.

For too many of us in this modern world, we're rapidly coming to a potential point of no return. If we don't act now and change, we may not be able to get out of the hole we've dug for ourselves. I'm not talking here about our natural environment, but of the health and happiness of humanity.

In this chapter, I run through some of the reasons we find ourselves in our current state, and introduce some of the methods I've devised for getting out of it.

How did we end up here?

I believe we are on a slippery slope for lots of reasons, but they really all come down to innovation. From the very beginning, humans have innovated, using fire for cooking, developing sharp tools for cutting, electricity for light and communication, and inventing many other creative and intelligent ways to make life easier and more enjoyable. However, it wasn't until the Industrial Revolution and the creation of the production line that human lifestyle really started to change dramatically.

Before then, most work required physical labour — kids worked in the fields alongside their parents and received rudimentary education. Food was organic, often plucked from the ground and processed by your own hands, or that of your neighbours. To get to school, work or social gatherings such as church or a barn dance, you either walked or rode a horse. You went to bed at sundown and woke up with the sunrise. Even in the cities, everything you needed was close by.

With the Industrial Revolution, manufacturing production lines started popping up everywhere. The only shortage was finding workers willing to swap fresh air and wide, open spaces for polluted and cramped city dwellings.

Thus, the modern schooling system was designed to equip children with an education and prepare them for jobs in the city. But, beneath the surface, it served another purpose — training the ideal production-line workers for the industrial age.

Even today, the structure of most classrooms reflects this outdated model. Instructions come from the front of the room, students sit in rows at their designated workstations, and bells dictate when to work, eat and go home. Questioning the curriculum is rarely encouraged. This setup may have served the needs of the past, but does it still serve the needs of the future?

With rapid advancements in technology, particularly AI, many traditional jobs are being automated, making much of what is taught today increasingly irrelevant. The real challenge now is whether our education system can evolve beyond this industrial-era framework. Will it equip students with the critical thinking, creativity and adaptability needed for a world where machines handle repetitive tasks? Or will it continue producing workers for a system that no longer exists?

When you add the creation of manufactured foods (those high in preservatives, sugar and many other harmful ingredients) to the rise of technology — where living someone else's life through a screen has become more important than your own — you can start to understand how society is losing the battle for health and happiness.

One of the other significant changes in our lifestyles is the way we receive our entertainment. Sometimes, I feel the days of our neighbourhoods being filled with activity — of sporting matches, kids climbing trees, parents helping to build and race billy carts, flying kites, playing marbles and every other wonderful game that kept kids outside until the sun went down — are numbered.

I wasn't a kid that long ago, but everyone I knew, as soon as we got home, ditched the school bag, grabbed a bite to eat, and then ran for our bike, skateboard, roller blades or surfboard. We wouldn't dream of re-entering the house until the sun went down.

Today, much of people's entertainment takes place within their homes, often through televisions, video games, tablets or smartphones. While this may seem like an exaggeration, statistics suggest otherwise — many individuals spend the equivalent of a full month each year watching TV[11] and upwards of eight hours a day in front of screens.[12] Combine this with a diet high in processed foods and low in nutritional value, and it's not hard to see why modern lifestyles are contributing to widespread health concerns.

My greatest concern, not just in Australia but globally, is that technology is keeping more and more people inside, being spectators rather than enjoying the great outdoors as participators. Once virtual reality becomes accessible and cheap enough for the everyday person, and is combined with online shopping, online streaming subscriptions and our growing addiction with gaming and social media, I'm concerned that our population will spend increasingly more time indoors, forgetting about the natural beauty and healing qualities that await them outside their front door. Already, our kids are spending less time outdoors than maximum security prisoners.[13]

If we want to reverse these trends, we need to start by rethinking how we engage with technology, food and daily movement.

Anti-social media: The paradox of connection

I recently had a very insightful conversation with my 15-year-old neighbour who's a very sporty and wholesome kid who seems, on the surface at least, to have it together and to not buy into the social media effect. I wanted to gain more insight into what was happening around the social media scene and how it affects teenagers psychologically. I already had a good idea from the research we'd done at GreenX7, but nothing is better for getting the lay of the land than a good old chinwag with a local.

I learned a lot from my neighbour during that chat, but the most impactful thing she said was about the effects of social media on teenagers. She told me, 'Your focus is on what other people think about you, and not what you think about yourself'.

Many teenagers feel pressure to live and present themselves in a certain way, often curating their lives to fit an idealised image — living what I call 'life through a lens'. Rather than embracing their individuality, many are drawn to mimicking influencers and personalities with cult followings on platforms such as Instagram, Facebook, Snapchat and TikTok. While this isn't true for all, the influence of social media has undeniably shaped the way many young people perceive themselves and the world around them.

My neighbour shared she was currently completing a school assignment on fear, where each student had to explore and write about their personal fears. To prompt discussion, the teacher presented images and clips of scary clowns, great white sharks, and extreme heights — classic examples of fears, but ones that rarely affect daily life. After all, encountering a menacing clown on the street or finding Jaws waiting at the top of an escalator is hardly an everyday occurrence.

Yet, the fears that impact many teenagers — and even adults — are far less dramatic but far more pervasive. One of the most common and deeply felt fears is the fear of judgement — the worry of how others perceive you, the pressure to meet expectations, and the anxiety of not being accepted. Unlike the exaggerated fears shown in class, this is a fear that follows teenagers through school halls, social media feeds and daily interactions, shaping their confidence and sense of self.

This feeds into the ideas Bronnie Ware outlines in her book *The Top Five Regrets of the Dying*. Based on her time spent caring for the dying in palliative care, Ware highlights the number one regret she heard was, 'I wish I'd had the courage to live a life true to myself, not the life others expected of me'.

This isn't just a throw-away sentence; behind this are layers of self-doubt, anxiety and depression that stop us from living a healthy and happy life.

What started in a dorm room back in 2004 and is now known as Facebook, part of Meta Platforms, has helped change the way we look at ourselves. As my neighbour said, 'Your focus is on what other people think about you and not what you think about yourself'. Through a device that sits in our hands, we can access a showreel of everyone's 'best moments' and, because this platform (and others like it) offers an endless scroll, we can be constantly bombarded with people doing cool stuff from every corner of the globe. Before social media, our fear of missing out (FOMO) might have been triggered by a chat over the back fence, and finding out your neighbour was going camping over the holidays. Now, it can be triggered almost constantly.

While social media has given us incredible ways to stay connected — allowing long-distance friendships to thrive and providing a lifeline for connection during times of isolation — it has also subtly changed the way we interact in person. These days, we often know what's happening in our friends' lives before we even meet up, thanks to the endless stream of updates at our fingertips.

This can sometimes take the excitement out of real-life conversations. When we do catch up, instead of sharing stories with fresh enthusiasm, we already know the punchlines, the highlights, and the latest events in each other's lives. And, ironically, while sitting together, we commonly find ourselves distracted, glancing at our phones to check in on what everyone else is doing, just in case we're missing out.

Social media has enriched our connections in many ways, but it's also worth being mindful of how it shapes our in-person interactions. Finding a balance between using it to stay connected while still being present in the moment can help us make the most of both worlds.

Innovation has undoubtedly made our lives more convenient, allowing us to enjoy comforts previous generations could only dream of. We've swapped bikes and horses for cars, automated everything from garage doors to TV channels, and can even have a meal prepared and delivered without ever stepping outside. Technology has given us incredible benefits — but it's also changed the way we interact with the world around us.

Family time, once filled with outdoor adventures and shared experiences, is now too often replaced by screens. Parents work harder to keep up with rising costs, while children are entertained with tablets and phones. Meanwhile, poor diets, a lack of meaningful connection and the habit of passively consuming life through screens are contributing to growing issues such as obesity, depression and a fading enthusiasm for life.

But here's the good news — we're not stuck on this path. The future isn't written, and we have the power to shift the direction we're heading. By being more intentional with how we spend our time and intentionally recharging our batteries, we can make room for what truly makes life fulfilling.

Reversing the trend

I had a great conversation with my brother, Sam, about what's holding people back from taking action to improve their wellbeing. As a police officer and a family man, I value his grounded perspective. Two things he said really stuck with me. Firstly, people need hope to make positive changes, not necessarily happiness. When you're overwhelmed or stuck, it's often hope, not joy, that keeps you moving forward. Secondly, people need something to move toward; a sense of purpose or a goal that gives their efforts meaning. In short, people need both the willingness and the belief that things can get better and that they are worth that effort. It's often the struggle itself that reveals this gap and becomes the call to action.

An example goal for him was to be an active parent; for someone who is single, the goal may be to attract a partner, or a working couple may want good health in retirement. Whatever the goal or purpose, it must be strong enough to make you really want to change, and to stay that way.

When I was talking with my brother, I had recently attended a talk by Paul Spinks, an advanced care paramedic. With an extensive background in trauma counselling, Spinks's talks focus heavily on how depression can lead to suicide and obesity, and how we are, in his words, 'micro-managing ourselves sick'.

Spinks presents real-life accounts from his own work experiences that highlight vividly the current state of mental health issues in Australia, and their effect on our wellbeing.

The following quick statistics presented by Spinks horrified me. Out of every 100 Australians, by the age of 65:

- 27 will be dead
- 68 per cent will be flat broke
- 50 per cent will have suffered a relationship breakdown
- 50 per cent will have suffered poor mental health
- 82 per cent will have a chronic illness.[14]

Which one of these statistics will you be? If it's not you, it's your partner, kids or a close friend or family member. Is this enough motivation for you to start reversing some of those bad habits for you and your family? To start helping your work colleagues do so?

When looking at those statistics, don't just read over them. Think about each one and what your life, and that of your family, would be like if even one of those was to creep in. If it already has — which, statistically, is very likely — what can you do to climb out of the hole, fill it back in, and cover it with concrete so it you don't repeat the process?

The unfortunate thing about these statistics is that being flat broke can lead to relationship separation, which can lead to poor mental health, which in turn can lead to poor diet and decreased exercise — ultimately potentially leading to chronic illness, depression and, for some, suicide.

To combat these health risks, so much of the health industry focuses on recovery and rehabilitation. However, from my lived experience working with rehabilitation centres and watching two brothers struggle for many years on both prescription and recreational drugs, I know that if we are ever going to solve our health crises, we have to look at a preventative framework, rather than wait for people to go into recovery — or never make it there in the first place.

I mention my interest in the UK's Green Social Prescribing (GRx) initiative in chapter 1. This focuses on prevention rather than cure, through the prescription of nature-based activities instead of traditional medication. And the results of this initiative have been promising. In a study from the University of Sheffield, including over 8300 individuals participating, many from disadvantaged backgrounds, showed that people who engage in green exercise report significant improvements in their mental wellbeing, including increased happiness and life satisfaction, along with reduced anxiety levels. In some cases, these improvements even exceeded national averages. The approach has also proven to be a cost-effective alternative to conventional treatments such as therapy, making it a viable long-term solution for supporting mental health. By reconnecting people with nature, this model is showing that simple, accessible solutions can have a profound impact on wellbeing.[15]

For me, reconnecting with nature can be just what people need to build those two vital ingredients and have both the willingness *and* the ability to look after themselves and strive for change — and the resilience to keep looking after their battery.

Finding resilience through wellness

Many people define resilience as 'toughness'. However, I don't believe 'toughness' is really about the Clint Eastwood, 'heart of stone', 'looks could kill' kind of toughness. Indeed, I've seen plenty of tough-looking people wilt when life situations get rough, and I've also seen individuals who appear meek and mild stand tall and strong in the face of adversity, time and time again. So, let's take the term 'tough' as meaning to be internally strong, and understand that building resilience is not about building muscles at the gym but rather flexing other 'muscles' in your mind, body and soul.

So, how do you build resilience — and how can you measure it?

I believe the two vital ingredients for wellness — the ability and the willingness — form the two sides of your resilience.

Willingness is your sheer determination to keep pushing, pulling, grabbing and grinding no matter what. It's your internal mindset that, no matter how big, wide or far the challenge, you have no other thought apart from 'just keep swimming, just keep swimming', just like Dory in *Finding Nemo*.

Of course, bad days, bad feelings and bad outcomes will always occur. But with the right mindset, these become just another obstacle to heave yourself over, hoping for sunshine on the other side. I've worked with people who feel like they're right at the edge, emotionally spent and unsure how to keep going. A phrase I hear more often than I'd like is, 'I just want to tap out,' as if life has become a fight they can no longer endure. But in most cases, it's not life they're trying to leave — it's the pain. It's the struggle they want to escape, not life itself. That expression isn't always a call to end it all, but more a desperate wish to make it all stop for a while. When you've lost someone to suicide and you've felt the ripple of heartbreak it leaves behind, all you want to do is reach out, hold on, and say, 'You don't have to tap out. Maybe you just need to tap off for a moment — to rest, to breathe, to feel safe.' If I could, I'd give them floaties and whisper, 'You just have to stay afloat until the tide changes.'

On the other side of this mindset is your ability — that is, the energy and vitality you have to tackle obstacles and challenges that are constantly put in your way. This is the energy you need to keep on getting up, every time you are pushed down.

Your willingness wants you to get up, and your ability allows you to do so.

I boxed for many years to release pent-up emotions. I would strap up my hands, put on the gloves and either beat up the bag or step into the ring and box out all those negative feelings. While I've found better ways to deal with my emotions, boxing is still a nice metaphor for resilience. You need to have the willingness and the ability to go again and again every time the bell rings — to step forward and confront what you know is going to hurt. Typically, the boxer with the most willingness (drive and hunger) and ability (the stamina to maintain their physical and technical ability) will win if evenly matched. Sometimes life throws you one or two rounds, and other times you must go toe to toe for 12 rounds while you feel your life force draining away.

As I outline in chapter 1, through my work with GreenX7, I've come to understand that certain areas in our lives help us maintain both our ability and willingness to keep throwing on the gloves and come out punching day after day, year after year. I've used these foundational pillars both personally and professionally with my clients at GreenX7, whether they are athletes, leaders or just people that want to succeed at becoming the best version of themselves. These foundational pillars support you in your deliberate efforts to look after yourself.

These areas are:

- purpose
- physical health
- mindset
- relationships

- sleep
- nutrition
- fun
- friendships

These eight areas determine your health, happiness, balance, connections and purpose, and the better you rate in each area, the better your overall resilience and wellbeing.

As shown in the following figure, when all these areas come together, they form your battery — the source of your energy, resilience and ability to take on whatever life throws your way. How full or depleted that battery is determines whether you're just surviving, merely functioning, or truly thriving.

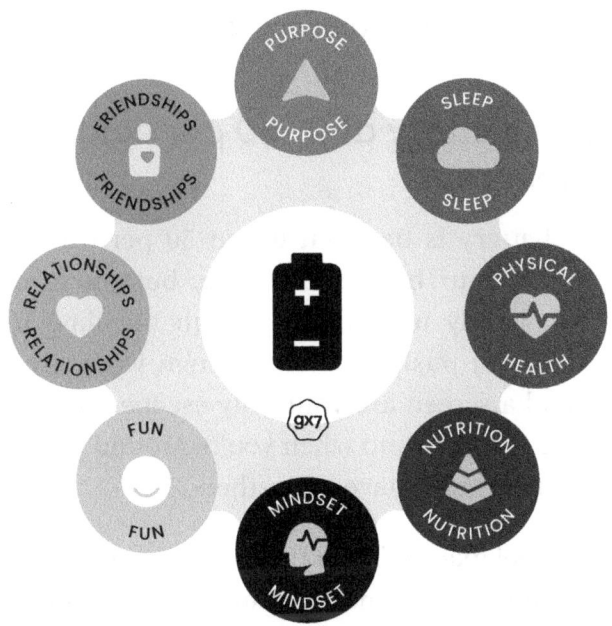

The eight wellness areas that make up your battery

The battery zones

Since 2017, we have measured thousands of batteries at GreenX7 to better understand how we can improve wellbeing. Our research spans individuals, organisations, industries and communities. What stands out is that across all our data points, the average battery level sits around 64 per cent. This means most people are simply functioning — getting through the day but not truly thriving.

This section runs through these battery zones to help you understand where you might currently stand. Just remember — your battery doesn't define who you are; it simply reflects your current wellbeing and energy levels at this moment in time. The good news is that through the remaining parts in this book, I focus on helping you build the habits that will recharge and sustain your energy.

Surviving (battery at 0–50 per cent): The zombie zone

When your battery is between 0 and 50 per cent, you're in survival mode. Your body is running, but you're operating on autopilot, barely making it through the day. You wake up exhausted and push yourself through work. By evening, the couch and a screen are your only escape. Life feels like a constant energy drain, and when you're around people, you're often just pretending to have it together.

At worst, you feel like you're on the verge of imploding — you're emotionally checked out and running on fumes. Your physical, mental and emotional reserves are dangerously low, and burnout is either here or just around the corner.

When I coach leaders through this phase, my focus is on breaking things down to rebuild, restoring energy, resetting habits, and finding the spark that's been lost.

Functioning (battery at 50–70 per cent): The cruise control zone

Most people live here. You're getting through life just fine — you look the part and you're doing what's expected — but inside, something feels off. You're in a repetitive cycle of waking up, working, getting some sleep, and then repeating it all over again.

The fun is missing, and you can't quite put your finger on why. You experience ups and downs, and moments where you feel good followed by slumps that make you wonder where your energy went. You might find yourself asking, 'Is this all there is?'

During this time I encourage leaders to focus on resetting and recharging, and making small but powerful changes that help them reclaim joy, purpose and momentum.

Momentum (battery at 70-79 per cent): The momentum zone

You're not just surviving or coasting anymore — things are starting to click. You've made some shifts, maybe reconnected to what matters, and there's a noticeable lift in your energy. You feel more present, more aware, and at times even optimistic. But you're not quite firing on all cylinders — yet.

It's a delicate stage where consistency matters. Some days you feel like you're thriving, and then a small stressor knocks you off rhythm. When I coach people here, we focus on strengthening routines, locking in new habits, and bridging the gap between momentum and mastery. This is the launchpad to the thrive zone.

Thriving (battery at 80 per cent and above): The thrive zone

This is where the magic happens. Only about 15 per cent of people consistently operate here, but when they do, they're unstoppable.

You wake up excited for the day. You have energy, drive and a deep sense of purpose. You're mentally sharp, emotionally resilient and physically strong. You radiate positivity, and people naturally gravitate toward your energy.

At this stage, you're not just getting through life; you're fully living it. Work, relationships and personal growth feel aligned, and even when challenges arise, you have the tools and mindset to handle them with confidence.

I remind leaders that the goal is sustainability, keeping that flow state alive and ensuring it becomes a way of life, not just a temporary peak.

Not everyone stays in the thrive zone 100 per cent of the time. Life throws curveballs through unexpected stress, setbacks and tough days. The difference is that when your battery is consistently high, your resilience is high — so you bounce back faster.

The goal — for you and your team — isn't just reaching the thrive zone once; it's about learning how to recharge quickly and stay there as much as possible.

At first, this takes effort. But once you start using the tools in this book, it becomes second nature. Thriving becomes your new normal. And best of all? You'll feel lighter, more energised and more connected to life than ever before.

Using a game of cards to create connection

As I outline in chapter 1, when we created the eight wellness areas and the GreenX7 tools, we were also looking for a way to measure and improve wellbeing. I realised that just asking someone, 'Are you okay?' and them saying they're 'fine', was not an accurate measuring tool. I must have asked my friend Mal that same question 100 different ways over the years, and the answer was always something along the lines of, 'I'm fine', 'I'm good', 'All good mate' or any other way that allows someone to brush the question off and keep plugging away. We knew the eight wellness areas that make up your battery were a powerful way to simplify and understand wellbeing. We just needed a way to get people to connect and create deeper conversations. We came up with the perfect solution: a game of cards. The magic of the game is that finally everything that's going on in your head, making you happy, sad, busy or frustrated, is laid out in front of you. The cards take all the white noise that makes up your life and rolls it out in two neat rows that are easy to digest. The figure on page 47 shows the eight cards that make up the game, which we called the 'Play for Your Life' cards. No doubt, you'll notice these are the same eight wellness areas that create health, happiness, balance and overall wellbeing, and make up your personal battery. These areas really decide our ups and downs — and the cards provide the opportunity to decipher them and understand how we got there.

When using the cards in workshops or presentations, or even one on one, I first ask someone to choose a card (or two cards) they're feeling good about, and then think about why they made this choice. I then ask them to choose a card they would like to improve on, and again think about why they made this choice. I also ask them to think about what they could do to make an improvement, and when they could start.

The more I played the game, the more I added, adjusted and perfected how the cards looked and what content I needed to add, not just to ask the questions but to also help people solve their own problems.

What I found was that most people knew what they needed to do — the card game simply allowed them to create the time and space to articulate this. Keep these cards in mind as you work through the chapters in the next part. I then take you through the full exercise in applying them to an area you'd like to improve in chapter 20. Once you have a better idea of all the areas that make up your battery — that is, the elements that fuel your wellbeing — the real question is how do you keep your battery charged? How do you ensure you're not just getting by but building the strength to take life's hits and keep moving forward? How do you inspire those around you to do the same? Like anything worth fighting for, keeping your battery fully charged requires intention and effort. You can't leave it to chance. This is where the GreenX7 tools come in — the focus of part III of this book.

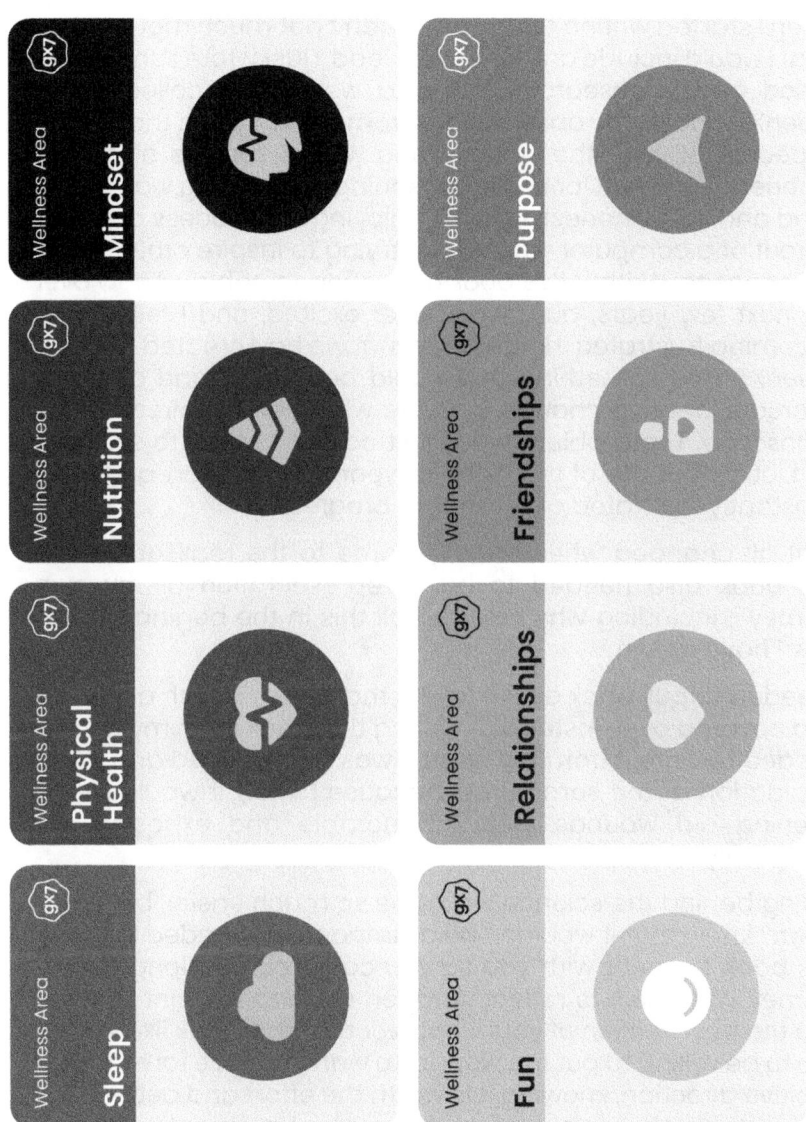

The GreenX7 Play for Your Life cards

Wellness Area
Mindset

Wellness Area
Purpose

Wellness Area
Nutrition

Wellness Area
Friendships

Wellness Area
Physical Health

Wellness Area
Relationships

Wellness Area
Sleep

Wellness Area
Fun

47

BEING GROUNDED, RESILIENT, OPEN AND WELL IN ORDER TO GROW

When I started writing this book, I hadn't put much thought into what I would include and where. Instead, I just wrote summaries based on the research and data we'd been collecting at GreenX7, added my observations from working with thousands of people all over the world, along with a sprinkle of my life experience in there for some seasoning. The writing was a slow grind and, to be honest, I wasn't enjoying the process of sitting in front of a computer when I was trying to inspire others to do the opposite. Writing this book continued to ebb and flow over the next few years, but I was never excited, and I felt myself becoming frustrated. I knew that what we had created through GreenX7 was something that could be shared and adopted to create positive change in those who were inspired by our philosophy. The problem was I just couldn't seem to sit down and let it pour out of me. Year on year, I would start and stop, constantly frustrated at my lack of progress.

That all changed when I finally came to the realisation that this book also needed to be a representation of my own journey — including why I started all this in the beginning and how I have grown.

I needed to pull back all the layers that the research and data had covered over. Instead of writing this book from my head, I needed to write it from my heart. I was both excited and full of trepidation at the same time, because I knew it would mean opening old wounds, being vulnerable and exposing my underbelly.

Hiding behind the science would be so much easier, but deep down I knew that it wouldn't be as impactful. I needed to make this book connect with you so you could come along on the journey with me — to reflect, to open up, and to want to grow into the best version of you, whatever that may look like. I need you to be willing to put the work in, to want to move forward in a positive direction, knowing it is worth the effort and better than being stuck where you are at this present moment. I needed you to want to grow — and to do that, I had to be real with myself and with you.

When I peeled back all the layers and started to change my focus, I realised an important truth. After years of thinking that I was creating this philosophy for everyone else, and developing a framework that has helped create a rhythm for everyday wellness for thousands of people around the world, I realised I was doing it for myself. I needed this framework just as much as anyone else. I was also hurting, I also needed to heal, and I also needed to grow into a better version of myself. Everything I have been creating, researching, observing and living since 2013 has been helping me to grow, and this was also what this book needed to be about — how to GROW, through being grounded, resilient, open and well.

With fresh eyes and an open heart, I looked back through my journals, scribbles, diary entries and reflections, and started to piece them all together. What I discovered was that all the tools we had created along the way amplified my want and need to grow. From the eight wellness areas and the Play for Your Life cards, to the GreenX7 tools and even the app, they were all purposefully created to move me along this journey, step by step. While I was helping others grow on their own journey, they were helping me grow on my own.

This book is about creating the time and space for you to just *be*, to do the things that make your heart sing so you can recharge your battery and be the best version of you. I've realised over all these years is that finding this space isn't selfish but the exact opposite — being the best version of me means that everyone else gets to share that as well. My wife, my kids, my family and friends, my staff and my clients all benefit from me being at the top of my game, both personally and professionally. I already know from all the research and data that the better my battery, the better I am in all areas of my life; when I sit in nature, my heart tells me too. And while in nature, far removed from the crap that is constantly fed to us through marketing and media, I also resonate more with my purpose — to inspire others to reconnect to themselves, others and the natural environment for everyday wellness.

Finally, I'm inspired through knowing exactly what has helped me to grow, and now I finally get to share it with you.

PART II

YOUR BATTERY

Keeping all the areas of your battery charged and working together is almost like sculpting a masterpiece. Just as a bodybuilder carefully trains each muscle for strength and balance, you need to fine-tune every aspect of your wellbeing to create a strong, sustainable foundation. This isn't about perfection; it's about progress. It's about making small, deliberate choices that add up to something powerful.

But effort without purpose fades fast. To stay committed, you need a reason why — a force greater than the grind. Maybe your reason is to be more present with your loved ones, to have the energy to pursue your passions, or to show up as the best version of yourself. Whatever it is, that why is what fuels the fire.

Throughout the next few chapters, we take a deeper dive into each of the areas that make up your battery — including why it matters, how it impacts your life, and what you can do to strengthen it. Because when you have a full battery, you don't just exist — you live. And you inspire others to also be the best versions of themselves. And that's the goal, isn't it? So let's start with your purpose.

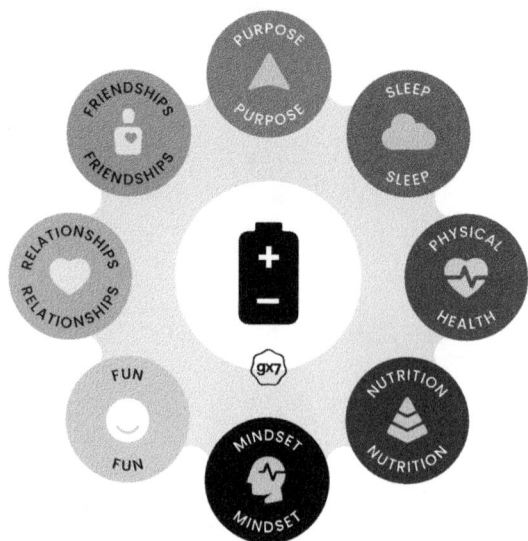

Chapter 3

Purpose

In the early days of creating the Play for Your Life cards, which I introduce in chapter 2, I visited the rehabilitation centre at the Tweed Hospital in northern New South Wales. By this stage, I knew the cards allowed people to open up and gain insights into areas in their life they would not normally talk about. I also knew just sitting there and actively listening to someone, creating a sense of value and belonging, was extremely powerful. So I set out the cards with a young man in front of me, desperately trying to give him 100 per cent of my attention; however, I was distracted by a woman walking around the courtyard talking on her phone. She was battered and bruised, and just seemed to have had the life sucked out of her. I realised everyone else at the rehabilitation centre seemed a bit the same, as they sat around and smoked while trying to soak up some sun and a little hope. As much as I was trying to be present with the young man in front of me, I couldn't help but also overhear the woman's conversation.

I had laid out seven of the eight cards, giving a brief description on each card as I went. In front of me were the cards of sleep, physical health, nutrition, mental health and attitude, fun, relationships and friendships. I was skipping over these because I knew none of these mattered for the man in front of me; he had hit rock bottom and was looking for a reason to live. I had come to the final card, my sole reason for being there. As I went to play the purpose card, I overheard the woman on the phone say, 'I know that I have not been a very good mum and I know that I have been a hopeless wife this year, but all I can think about right now is how long that piece of rope needs to be to hang myself with'.

I stopped with the purpose card mid-air in my hand, her words hitting me with a sudden jolt. I knew what the back of the purpose card said, and I knew right there and then that these words could have a detrimental effect on the young man I was in front of. Those card words were, 'What can you do with your strengths, values and passions to help others?' Here I was, sitting in a rehab centre with a man who himself was in survival mode — and I'm about to ask him what he can do to help others?

That experience changed the way I looked at purpose. Instead of asking people to consider what they can do to help others, I changed the card to read, 'Our foremost purpose in life is to look after and value ourselves mentally, physically and emotionally. From here, we can look at how we are able to utilise our strengths, passions and values to help and inspire others'.

In that moment, I very much realised the significance of making sure we fill up our own cup first, so we had something to share and are able to help others.

The young man sitting opposite me that day was my little brother.

Finding your purpose

Having run wellbeing workshops all over the world, I know that the culture, country, psychographic or demographic I'm presenting to doesn't matter. Wherever I am, less than half of my audience would say they have a strong purpose — that is, a distinct purpose that they wake up with every morning, knowing what they want to do with their life and, most importantly, why. What I've seen through coaching is that if people don't feel like they have a purpose, they tend to drift. If they don't have a strong enough *why*, they don't have the motivation to prioritise their own wellbeing.

Typically, most of us think about purpose as outward-looking, with a focus on helping others, which is a good thing. However, I believe that our primary purpose needs to be to look after ourselves. This is selfless — rather than selfish — because we can't give from an empty cup. You can't be the best version of yourself with an empty battery — and you surely don't want to be the one to end up needing help because you pushed yourself to breaking point.

If you commit to recharging your battery every day, then no matter what you're doing, no matter what path you're on, you will always be on purpose. As you recharge, you become the best version of yourself and start to thrive sustainably. This, in turn, inspires and encourages others, and has a positive impact on all your relationships.

Once you are thriving sustainably, you will have the energy to uncover your strengths, passions and beliefs, and how you can use these to help others. You can then combine them to formulate a more defined purpose. My personal purpose is 'to inspire others to reconnect to self and others through nature'.

I do this through many pathways, whether it's speaking, coaching, consulting or just being there for someone.

Rather than asking yourself, 'What can I do?', consider first asking yourself, 'What kind of person do I want to be? What qualities, values, strengths and passions do I appreciate in myself and others?'

When you can find the things that are important to you — and not just what others expect of you — you can contribute to making those things happen. You become part of a greater community and feel you are contributing to something outside of yourself. This helps you feel connected and valued, and improves your self-worth.

To help find your purpose, ask yourself these important life questions:

- Why do I want to be the best version of myself?
- What or who am I really doing it for?
- What kind of person do I want to be?

Prioritising yourself — and then others

When we talk about wellbeing and wellness, we are talking about two different things. Wellbeing means 'to be in a comfortable state — mentally, emotionally, physically and spiritually'. Wellness means 'to make the deliberate effort to nurture your wellbeing'.

You really do have to prioritise yourself first to make sure you can continue to thrive sustainably and give the best version of yourself to others. I'm sure you are aware of the two versions of yourself — the one where you are full of energy and life, nothing seems to bother you and everyone enjoys being around you, and the one where you feel like you are just surviving and everything seems to get on your nerves. This version of you gets frustrated easily, and even the simplest roadblocks feel like you're trying to move heaven and earth — and that's just trying to open the strawberry jam jar!

Being kind to yourself isn't just a nicety; it's your birthright and, if you're not already, you need to get good at it. If you don't have enough self-worth or self-love, you won't have the motivation to make that deliberate effort to want to look after yourself.

Next time you're looking in the bathroom mirror, look at yourself — really look at yourself — deep into your eyes as if you're admiring a beautiful work of art. When you've connected with yourself, say, 'I see you'. And keep saying it until it registers, until you feel it deep in your heart and you truly believe it. You're worthy.

I am also enamoured by the Japanese philosophy of Kaizen. It's a philosophy focused on making small, continuous improvements over time to achieve long-term success.

The core idea is that small, incremental changes lead to major improvements, and this can be implemented both personally and professionally.

Finding your purpose at work — and with your team

Having a strong purpose in your work life brings a higher energy to your team and the projects you work on. When your purpose and personal values, and those of your team, align with company values, you all gain greater satisfaction and engagement.

One word of caution here: you do have to be careful of not using all your purpose and energy on work, and having nothing left in the tank for yourself and others.

A great example is a client of mine in the childcare industry who has a direct impact on over 5000 families. Their leadership team are so pumped with their vision and current projects, and the opportunity to create positive change that they constantly give 110 per cent. We just have to make sure that they have balance and can continue to thrive sustainably. Just remember — you're no help to anyone when you can't get out of bed.

Consider the following ways to bring purpose to yourself and your team at work:

- *Ensure your personal and company values align:* If you're a greenie at heart and working for an oil company, for example, it might be time to move on. Make sure that you and everyone in your team resonates with your workplace.

- *Move from macro to micro:* Understand the big picture and the mission at play, and then help your team work towards micro goals each day that bring this mission to life.

- *Grow:* Continually look for ways for you and your team to feel like you're moving forward in the right direction.

- *Find your helpers high:* When you assist others, your brain releases neurotransmitters such as dopamine and endorphins, which are associated with pleasure and reward. This can lead to feelings of euphoria and contentment. So help your team also find their purpose.

TAKING ACTION

Let's make purpose practical.

PURPOSE TIPS

- Start with you — to find your purpose, you need to find yourself first.

- Understand what makes your heart sing.

- Live a life true to yourself and not from others' expectations.

- Use your strengths, passions and, most importantly, your values to find your purpose.

- Make a deliberate effort to recharge your batteries each day so you have the vitality to live your purpose from your fullest potential.

TIME FOR ACTION QUESTIONS

- If you were to name this chapter in your life, what would the title of this chapter be?

- What is your intention/what matters most here?

- How would you know you were making progress? What would you need to prioritise?

LET'S MAKE IT HAPPEN!

Take one minute now to write down the kind of person you wish to be, and then set an intention to do one thing today to move towards being this person. Lock it in and recharge your own battery.

TESTIMONIAL: FINDING A PURPOSE

I went to see Tim as a last resort, to be honest. I was suffering from depression, loneliness, disconnection with self and just overall low motivation. All I really knew of Tim was that he was the turtle guy who couldn't stop smiling — it's seriously infectious, actually.

Tim's first coaching session with me was us perched up the sand dunes hanging out in two hammocks, just having a chat. I felt zero judgement when sharing my story and just an ease to the whole approach. There were tough questions, along with some tears and many laughs. We started with a few simple everyday changes that I was going to implement into my routines. It was a gentle and easy way to get started. As we continued to meet across the following few weeks, I had to complete modules — things like, 'What are your strengths?' and 'List your top five values' and 'What is your purpose?'

It sounds like easy work, but I really struggled. I realised this was not because I didn't have any values or a purpose, but because I couldn't see them. Through further conversations, reflection and Tim's help, I began to see.

In our last session, I found out what my purpose was and how I was going to live it. In that session, I felt so connected to my five values and who I am. I felt an overwhelming sense of closeness and ease with myself, something I had never felt before. I now know that wherever I am on this journey we call life, I can come back to my values to make decisions. I can remind myself what my purpose is, and I can come back to my strengths and passions when I feel lost. Or I can simply just take a breath.

Tim told me, 'Only when you take off your mask can you truly find out who you are and where you want to go'. Tim helped me take off my mask, and I will forever be deeply grateful.

Iness Heywood

Chapter 4

Sleep

Prior to having children, I was a sleeping machine; it would be fair to say that if sleeping was a sport, I'd have a cabinet full of trophies. I was in bed by 9.00 pm on most nights, and up at 4.30 am the next morning, full of beans and getting stuff done while waiting for the rest of the world to wake up. Whenever I facilitated a keynote or workshop, I'd ask the audience who was struggling to get their seven to eight hours of quality sleep each night. Inevitably, half the audience would raise their hands — and I'd just say, 'Do better'.

I've now got two kids under four and if someone asked me if I get seven to eight hours of good-quality sleep, I would laugh out loud and ask them what kind of sick joke they were playing at!

Each night now becomes a battlefield. Carly and I don our war paint, look at each other with grit, determination and worry lines, and say, 'Good luck'. Before kids, we would have said, 'Good night, sweet dreams'.

But it's when Carly is on her night shifts as a firefighter that my trauma starts to really kick in. Let me lay out a typical evening routine with kids for you, if you don't have the 'privilege' of experiencing it:

- *4.30 pm:* Pick the kids up from kindy (hangry and highly emotional).

- *4.30 to 5.00 pm:* Play in the park to release any excess energy.

- *5.00 pm:* Walk in the door to the tune of 'I want a banana' on repeat while trying to sort dinner.

- *5.00 to 5.30 pm:* Still listening to 'I want a banana' and 'play Moana soundtrack' while trying to calmly keep the kids away from hot boiling water and telling them to 'play outside'.

- *5.30 to 6.00 pm:* Eat dinner (picture a hyena and a monkey eating together who think their sole purpose is to put more food out and around their mouth rather than into it).

- *6.00 to 6.30 pm:* Bath time (similar to dinner time, just now with water).

- *6.30 to 7.30 pm:* Kids have downtime while I clean up ('downtime' is a very loose term for 'anything can happen at this point').

- *7.30 to 7.45 pm:* Bedtime routine — teeth, read books and Sonny goes to sleep (he's made it through the dark side).

- *7.45 to 8.45 pm:* FRANKIE! As I said in chapter 1, thank goodness she's cute.

- *8.45 pm to 5.00 am:* The battlefield — let's just say if I've only woken up four times to 'put on a sheet', 'water',

'I want to sleep in your bed', 'banana' (and so on), then I'm winning.

Still striving for better sleep

What my kids have shown me is that if I don't get good-quality sleep, I struggle to have energy to move my body the next day and I emotionally eat crappy foods. This all combines to then affect my attitude — and my negative attitude can have an impact on all facets on my personal and professional life. So whether it's due to kids, pets, or physical or mental injuries, if you're in an environment that's not conducive to good sleep, I feel you.

However, that doesn't mean you have a hall pass to give up trying — because better sleep gives you a better life.

Sleep is the foundation of the wellness areas — without sleep, you won't have the energy to improve your other areas. So you need to establish this foundation before moving on to the other areas in your personal battery.

When you sleep your body regenerates itself, refreshing the mind and repairing the body. With adequate sleep, your mind and body can function at their best. For the adult human body, 'adequate' means between seven and eight hours of uninterrupted sleep each night (and teenagers need more). Creating a sleep routine where you go to bed and wake up at consistent times will help set up your day for improved wellbeing. I know — if you have young kids or do shift work, this is more challenging, but having a daily rhythm you are aiming for still helps. (When Carly works her night shifts, for example, I see how much harder she must work to get quality sleep, and that she may need a siesta here and there.)

We are all born with our own circadian rhythm, and this can be hard — but not impossible — to change. Some of us are night owls and others are morning larks. However, try to factor into your rhythm that sleeping between 8 pm and midnight offers the best chance for restorative sleep, because these hours align with when the body is naturally more primed for deep sleep stages.[16] I know it can be tempting to watch just one more episode of your favourite Netflix series, but if it throws your whole routine out, you need to ask yourself whether it's worth it.

If you're constantly going to bed late and feeling tired when you wake up, it's a pretty clear indication that you need to hit the hay earlier. This may mean looking at your nightly routine and seeing how you could trim down some of your screen time.

Your focus needs to be on building a life that supports you — rather than one you have to support. You don't want a life that makes you feel continually overwhelmed and exhausted. You need to create a rhythm and then set boundaries to make sure that your cup gets filled up first. You need to recharge your battery, starting with quality sleep, so you can be the best version of yourself each day, both personally and professionally.

Working better on quality sleep

Quality sleep is also essential to performing effectively for work. Adequate rest enhances cognitive functions, emotional regulation, decision making, and overall health.[17]

Consider the following ways you — and your team — can nurture yourself and feel more alert while at work:

- *Power naps:* If possible, having a short nap (between 10 and 20 minutes) can restore alertness without making you feel groggy. I normally have one after lunch.

- *Sunlight and fresh air:* Exposure to natural light helps regulate your circadian rhythm and improve mood. Throw in some movement as well.

- *Cold water splash and hydration:* Splash your face with cold water or drink a glass of water to wake up. Dehydration also worsens fatigue, so keep a water bottle at your desk.

- *Deep breathing exercises:* Try box breathing (inhale four seconds, hold four seconds, exhale four seconds, hold four seconds) to refresh the mind.

- *Stretching and movement:* Simple desk stretches, standing or a quick walk can re-energise the body.

- *Meditation or mindfulness breaks:* A five-minute mindfulness session can reduce fatigue and improve focus.

- *Tackling high-focus tasks first:* Work on the most challenging tasks when your energy is highest.

- *Alternating tasks to stay engaged:* Shift between different types of work to maintain engagement.

- *Protein and healthy fats:* Eat balanced snacks with high protein and healthy fats, such as nuts, yoghurt or eggs, to stabilise energy levels.

TAKING ACTION

Set yourself up for success by ensuring you get good-quality sleep each night.

SLEEP TIPS

- Create set times to go to bed and wake up.
- Have a wind-down and wake-up routine.

(continued)

- View daylight within 30 minutes of waking.

- Disconnect from screens an hour before going to bed.

- Have a dark room with fresh air when possible, and at 18°C is ideal.

- Eat earlier at night to allow time for your food to digest. At least two hours prior to getting horizontal.

- If you have a 'monkey mind' that doesn't switch off, try meditating before bed.

- Read a book while in bed to help you fall asleep.

- When you wake up, don't look at a screen for at least 30 minutes.

- Move throughout the day.

TIME FOR ACTION QUESTIONS

- What time do you need to go to sleep at night and wake up in the morning to feel energised?

- What is your perfect sleep routine? (Write this down.)

- What's one luxury you could afford yourself when you wake before life takes over?

LET'S MAKE IT HAPPEN!

Take one minute to set an intention to do one thing today or this week to improve your sleep. Lock it in! Recharge your battery.

Chapter 5
Physical health

I wish I could say that I'm ripped and run marathons, do 24-hour adventure races, have climbed Mount Everest and that motivational speaker (and retired United States Navy SEAL) David Goggins has my photo pinned on his bedroom wall as his inspiration to 'Do Better'. But, in all honesty, my greatest physical feat is holding my breath for over five minutes and that's more mental than physical (more on this in chapter 17). Yes, I do stay in shape but that's purely because I want to live a long and healthy life, and it only comes from my outdoor water sport pursuits and walking the dog. I've never really been one for gyms or pounding the pavements — for me, movement has to be fun.

My wife, Carly, on the other hand, is a weapon — a six-foot, lean, running machine who loves triathlons and competing in iron woman events such as the Coolangatta Gold. For her, running is fun. If you give us both an hour of free time, Carly will lace up and go for a run and I'll grab a paddle and play.

Finding what works for you

I personally don't believe that you need to pursue unenjoyable exercises to stay in shape. For me, it's all about finding something you love that raises your heartbeat, and then do it often. ('Lifetime' sports, such as tennis, are a great example of this. Through their combination of movement, coordination and connection — and their cultural propensity towards long-term participation — studies have shown that these lifetime sports can extend your life span by up to 10 years.[18])

Physical health is about how well your body works and how you feel. It's not about how you look; it is your vitality for life. When you have good physical health, you wake up in the morning with enthusiasm and motivation to move and make the most out of our day.

To live a long, healthy and happy life, you need to maintain a level of physical health that allows you to fulfil your daily and life goals. If you're living with physical health problems, such as chronic disease or pain, you are at much greater risk of developing anxiety or depression — so it's much better to look at prevention. This is where your ability and willingness come into play — I could very easily 'do nothing', for example, and start falling into the trap of being sedentary and emotionally eating. Soon enough, my battery would start to plummet — but I've been there before and I'm not willing to go there again, especially when I have overactive children on my hands.

The thing is if you haven't moved in a while, it's very hard to find the motivation to get started — similar to the concept of inertia (which is the tendency of an object to stay as it is, whether at rest or in motion). This concept reminds me of my first car, a little white Datsun sedan I bought for $300. Each morning I would have to use the choke just to get it warmed up — it was almost like it was sitting there thinking *Do I really want to put my joggers on?* But once the car got moving, she purred, and it felt really good. Movement creates movement; the more you move, the more you want to keep moving — and once you do, just like with my little Datsun, it feels really good.

Bringing physical health to work

Another reason my physical health is so important is because I know the benefits it has on my work life, and especially on my productivity and creativity. And to be at peak performance, I know I have to move my body.

Post-lunch, I notice that my brain activity starts to decline. I could just sit at my desk, staring at a blank screen or notepad, but I'm only kidding myself if I think I'm going to do good work. The term for this is *presenteeism* — being physically present but performing below your best. Instead, I know that moving my body is a wonderful way to bring my brain back online.

So I've built a daily habit to go and move my body after lunch — perhaps through a walking meeting, gym with a work buddy or a beach swim if I'm working from the home office.

Consider the following to put more movement into your work day for you and your team:

- *Commute using movement:* Try walking or cycling to work, for example. This is good for you and good for the environment.

- *Walk and talk:* Whether it's face to face or a conversation on your phone, make a habit of moving meetings.

- *Arrange some 'play dates':* Collect some work mates and find a collective hobby over a long lunch, such as going for a jog or to the gym, or simply going for a walk in the park.

- *Use the stairs:* If this is an option in your building, use the stairs instead of the lift every time you arrive and leave.

- *Set up a post-work workout:* Getting in some sort of activity before going back home after work can boost your energy to bring positives vibes into the household.

All of these activities can enhance cognitive function, reduce stress, increase energy and productivity, reduce health risks and loneliness, and improve longevity[19] — benefits enough on their own, but even better if you're getting paid for it!

One of the most important factors in all of this is modelling good behaviours to your team. As an example of this, I was recently on a Zoom chat with a very inspiring CEO who heads up a statewide department. This very busy leader is aspiring to create positive systemic change across her department through preventative health measures. One of her workplace initiatives is to allow all her staff an hour over lunch to do something that will improve their wellbeing — and she makes sure this happens by kicking everyone out (weather permitting) and locking the door!

TAKING ACTION

Get started on improving your physical health today.

PHYSICAL HEALTH TIPS

- Lock in a daily time that fits in with your routine.
- Remember — if it's fun, it gets done.

- Don't go too hard, too fast (to avoid doing yourself an injury).

- Grab your friend, partner or pet to keep you motivated.

- Make the activity easily accessible, so you can't use the 'it's too hard' excuse.

- Mix it up between low and high intensity (remembering you do need to get your heart rate up and sweat it out every now and again).

- Do your activity outdoors wherever possible to benefit from your natural environment.

TIME FOR ACTION QUESTIONS

- How would you rate your energy, vitality and enthusiasm to move?

- What can you do each day for your physical health?

- How could you incorporate this into your workday?

LET'S MAKE IT HAPPEN!

Take one minute to set an intention to do one thing today or this week to look after your physical health. Put it in your diary, phone a friend and lock it in! Recharge your battery.

Chapter 6
Nutrition

Before my 30s, the only reason I ate food was because it tasted good. I had no idea of the nutritional value of food, or how it affected my body or mind. I would buy pizzas, meat pies and iced coffees whenever I felt like it. If it tasted good, you ate it — right?

I only started thinking about these things one day at smoko (otherwise known as morning tea), when I was sitting with my meat pie, ice coffee and the *Gold Coast Bulletin* (a habit from my labouring days) and the following conversation with one of my staff took place. They said to me, 'Hey Tim, how does that food feel when you eat it?'

'Hmmm, I eat it because it tastes good.'

'Yeah, but what does your belly and brain feel like after you've eaten it?'

I was confused — I only ever ate food for the taste, not for the way that it made me feel. But the question made me think. For the first time in my life, I started to associate foods with the way I felt after eating them, and not just with how they tasted. This made me re-evaluate my relationship with food and really consider what I was putting in my body. From that moment on, I became empowered to make better decisions about how I wanted to feel.

This is why it's so important to not multitask while eating — so you can understand your brain and body's reactions to the foods you're feeding them.

Eat the foods that make you feel good — simples

Most people have some general knowledge about what constitutes a healthy diet and how eating well can help their overall health. What, how and when we eat can make a big difference to how our body processes food. Through science, we are also starting to realise the importance of the gut–brain connection.

Your gut and brain are in constant communication through the gut–brain axis, a complex system that links your digestive system to your nervous system. This connection means that what happens in your gut can influence your mood, stress levels and even cognitive function — all thanks to the vagal nerves (the main nerves of your parasympathetic nervous system), gut microbiota, and various neurotransmitters produced in your digestive tract. A healthy gut can contribute to a healthier mind, which is why diet and gut health play such a big role in mental wellbeing.

If you want your brain and body to work well, you need to make sure you're eating foods that are good for you. We are all different — some of us work better on a vegetarian diet, some of us on a Paleo diet and some of us on the seafood diet. (You know the one — 'If I see food, I eat it'. Sorry, dad joke.) The food that's right for you may not be the same as that chosen by your partner or your friends, so trying to force yourself to eat like them may not be the right fit for you. Personally, I love eating carbs but, unfortunately, bread and pasta don't love me as much and leave me feeling tired and bloated.

You can try a few different ways to find out what food groups work best for you, including — and most importantly — seeing a dietitian. However, the following quick exercise is a good place to start.

When you start to eat or drink something, stop everything you're doing and be present. Put your phone away, turn off your computer and eat with mindfulness. Just be in the moment, not doing anything else.

Then, take a moment to reflect and ask yourself, 'How do I feel after eating this food? Does this food make me feel energised or does it make me feel tired and sluggish?' Simple stuff, right, but how often are you doing it?

I realised a few years ago that my gut becomes bloated and my brain becomes more sluggish after eating gluten and dairy. Now, that wasn't good for me because I love croissants and coffee! I try now to choose carefully when I eat these foods. If I'm about to do a keynote or workshop where I need to be at my peak performance, I know I need to eat foods that give me energy and help me to feel light on my feet — foods such as granola and yoghurt for breakfast or a meat protein, quinoa and salad for lunch. If you know certain foods aren't so good for you, only eat them in moderation and at the times when your performance won't be affected.

Scientific studies have for a long time shown that a well-balanced diet can provide a range of health benefits that are fundamental to our wellbeing, the prevention of disease and our ability to thrive. But, honestly, you shouldn't need science to know that you should feel good in your body. I'm guessing if you spent a minute now you could name off a few foods that you know are best left untouched in your hidey hole — and, I hate to break it to you, but I'm throwing alcohol into this mix!

I just had a flashback from when I was staying at a fancy health retreat running a workshop. I was in the bathroom in my cabin looking under the sink and discovered, tucked away behind the drainage pipes, a whole bunch of 'contraband' — such as chocolate, chips, coffee satchels and lollies. Why do I bring this up? Because whoever had stashed them there wasn't ready to go 'cold turkey' and sometimes it's better to take small steps than go full force and regress.

Healthy eating at work

At this stage (hopefully) you're most likely thinking about how you can make better nutrition choices at home. However, let's not forget about work because you also need to eat there too! And your good choices can definitely rub off on your team around you.

Here are some tips to help you and your team at work:

- *Pack a healthy lunch box:* This will help you avoid going for the fast-food option and also give you more time to relax and enjoy your food while being present.

- *Don't multitask at your desk and scoff down your food:* This triggers a stress response, leading your body to store more fat.[20] When you're stressed, your body releases cortisol, a hormone that can increase appetite and promote fat storage, leading to what's sometimes called 'stress belly'.

  Avoid emotionally eating and instead go move your body: Moving your body gives you the same hit of dopamine as eating those tempting treats, helping to boost your mood. The big difference is physical activity also helps improve overall physical health and self-esteem, and reduces the risk of chronic diseases. In contrast, habitual emotional eating can lead to weight gain, feelings of guilt and potential health issues.[21]

- *Try not to eat alone:* You may have heard the saying, 'It's better to eat a pizza with friends than a salad alone'. Research indicates that sharing meals with others can enhance happiness and life satisfaction, while eating alone can lead to depression, poor sleep quality and accelerated cognitive decline.[22]

In summary—take a healthy packed lunch to work, find a friend, leave tech behind, walk to your favourite green space and enjoy the connection while getting some fresh air and sunshine. Encourage everyone on your team to do the same.

TAKING ACTION

Eat your way to healthy while enjoying the mood and performance benefits.

NUTRITION TIPS

- Listen to your body.
- If you're going to eat the 'bad' foods, choose your time wisely, grasshopper.
- Don't multitask (step away from your desk).
- Eat everything in moderation.
- Invite your friends and make a picnic of it (without your phones).
- Make a snappy snack pack so you're not always getting takeaway.
- Buy fresh, local produce where possible.

TIME FOR ACTION QUESTIONS

- What can you do to improve your nutrition?
- What are some foods or drinks you know you should avoid?
- Where's a green space near your home or workplace where you could enjoy the chance to 'disconnect and reconnect'?
- Who could join you?

LET'S MAKE IT HAPPEN!

Take one minute to set an intention to do one thing to improve your nutrition for today or this week. Put it in your diary, phone a friend and lock it in! Recharge your battery.

Chapter 7
Mindset

I had a problem with getting 'hangry'. Perhaps you've experienced this too — that colloquial 'disorder' where, when you become hungry, on the flip of a switch, you can also turn angry. If you can relate to this, I don't need to explain any further. If you (like my wife) can't comprehend what I'm saying, let me just say it could be due to low blood sugar levels — or perhaps there is no logical explanation.

I know it's not actually a disease or a disorder, although I did think it was genetic — and my 'hangriness' could certainly turn an amazing moment into 'Armageddon' within just a few minutes.

I told myself I needed to eat at intervals of around two hours — at 6.15 am, 8.30 am, 11.00 am and so on — and, if I didn't, you wouldn't want to be around me. I would get agitated, light-headed and unable to make rational decisions — to the point where I could be standing in front of a buffet of goodness, and still couldn't decide what to eat first. Simply put, when I was hangry, I certainly wasn't being the best version of myself.

This all came to a head pre-kids, when Carly and I were holidaying in Queenstown, New Zealand. We were chasing that iconic, melt-in-your-mouth, king size steak that the country is known for. We got all dressed up, walked out of our hotel and went straight to the well-known Botswana Butchery. We were so excited — Carly and I don't enjoy many things more than a great steak. When the waiter greeted us, I asked for his best table for two but, unfortunately, we were turned away because they were fully booked!

With heavy hearts, we tried all the other restaurants in town — all were fully booked out. Meanwhile, my attitude was sinking deep into despair and my hangry was rising like an ocean storm. Eventually, Carly asked what I wanted to do. I snapped at her in response, and our night continued downhill from there.

Moving on from a fixed mindset

My predisposition of getting hangry had turned a night that was supposed to be glorious into one that was bordering hell on earth. I had reached rock bottom with my shenanigans, and they were causing a rift between Carly and I. I realised I needed to change. I needed to change my mindset.

When I retold the events of that night to my mate Dave, he mentioned the book *Mindset: The New Psychology of Success* by Dr Carol Dweck. This book taught me that my hangriness wasn't a genetic flaw, but an attitude flaw. I realised that over many, many years, my belief had been fixed that 'I get hangry when I don't eat' — and so I got hangry when I didn't eat. I had to flip the switch, change my attitude and retrain my neurons to fire differently. In other words, I had to adopt a growth mindset.

It took me three months, but I went from needing to eat at 6.15 am, and around every two hours thereafter, to now intermittent fasting. I had taken my worst trait (okay, that's debatable; I have others) and, by using an attitude of gratitude, had turned it into an accomplishment.

What I realised when reading *Mindset* is that I thought my thoughts and attitudes had been stuck in a holding pattern. However, I now know my mindset can change and grow, and I can create new neurons to change how I act, feel and perceive — and that is a game changer. Now I just need to rid myself of my impatience!

Mindset and mental health

Our mental health and attitude are the keys for us being able to live a successful and happy life. If we don't look after our mental health, everything else goes by the wayside.

Mental illness is a widespread issue in Australia, affecting approximately one in five adults aged 16 to 85 each year. According to Australia's Black Dog Institute, the most common conditions include anxiety (affecting around 14 per cent of the population), depression (6 per cent) and substance use disorders (5 per cent). These disorders often overlap. For instance, someone experiencing anxiety may also develop depression, or a person struggling with depression might turn to alcohol or drugs as a way to cope. Of those experiencing mental illness in any given year, around 11.5 per cent have a single disorder, while 8.5 per cent face two or more. Over the course of a lifetime, nearly half of Australians will experience some form of mental illness.

Suicide remains a critical concern, with at least nine Australians losing their lives to suicide daily and around 30 more making an attempt. It is the leading cause of death for individuals aged 25 to 44 and the second leading cause for those aged 15 to 24 — making it a more significant threat than skin cancer.[23]

Despite the prevalence of mental health disorders, access to treatment remains a significant challenge. The Black Dog Institute also highlights that more than half of those affected do not seek professional help, often due to difficulties in early detection and diagnosis. The rate of people receiving treatment for mental illness is only half that of those with physical health conditions, highlighting a critical gap in mental health care and support.

Our mental health is made up of our emotional, psychological and social wellbeing. It can have a positive or negative effect on our overall mindset, and how we think, feel and act. When we have good mental health, we wake up each morning looking forward to the day ahead and have joy for life. But the opposite is also true — when we have ill mental health, just the very thought of having to leave your bedroom could have you shaking with anxiety.

Taking small steps to a more positive mindset

A client of mine hadn't left her home for three weeks and could barely leave her bedroom due to paralysing depression. When we connected, she told me her mind was like a deep dark cave and she was stuck at the very depths of despair, not knowing how to climb out. She had not even been able to clean the house in all that time. At the time, I had only just got into coaching and was only really starting to understand the full impact that depression can have on people and those around them.

A mutual friend had introduced this client to our Play for Your Life cards and GreenX7 tools (which I talk more about in part III), and I received a very uplifting email from her a week later.

On the back of the GreenX7 tool card for time (covered in chapter 15) the action step is, 'Take one minute to set an intention for what you want the next hour to look like for you'.

This client told me that card really resonated with her. The very first thing she did was to vacuum the house. When she finished, she read the card again and did the laundry; when she read the card again, she did the dishes. She lived her life one hour at a time but at that time of her life that was all she had the capacity to focus on. She says she now keeps that one card with her at all times and, when she gets stuck, she reads that one line.

Perhaps you've heard the proverb, 'The only one way to eat an elephant is one bite at a time'. Everything in life that seems daunting, overwhelming, and even impossible can be accomplished gradually by taking on just a little at a time.

Our mental health and attitude set our sails for the day ahead and have a major impact on the way we experience our life. The good news for most of us is we can choose the attitude that we are going to wake up with each day.

The term 'mental health' has gained a negative connotation, so I prefer using the word 'mindset' when looking at improving how we think, feel and act. Thinking about your mindset also helps you to understand how you can change a negative into a positive.

Think about a habit or limiting belief that may be holding you back, or affecting part of your life or relationships. Maybe you can think of a few; maybe your list is as long as your shopping list, which is where I was many moons ago. The important thing to understand is that if that habit or belief is causing you pain and you want to change, then it is possible — just like eating an elephant one bite at a time.

All I want you to do is choose a task or something that you may not be looking forward to today. Instead of thinking, *I have to do this today*, change your mindset to, *I get to do this today*. In Australia, most of us are relatively privileged, and get to do things some people could only dream of. For example, say you're thinking, *I don't want to go shopping today* — imagine how many people in the world can only dream of arriving at a place where food lines the shelves and they can choose anything they want! It would be like arriving at Willy Wonka's Chocolate Factory!

You can also look at this from a work perspective. Perhaps you don't want to pitch for that new client or deal with that annoying staff member. Everything you have done and achieved throughout your life has led you to being in this exact position right now in your life. Think about the blood, sweat and tears to get you to where you are — only for you to now say, 'I don't want to'.

Change your perspective because you have the ability to do so. Tell yourself, 'I get to shop and put food on the table', 'I get to pitch to a new client and show them what I'm capable of', 'I get to work with so many different people with unique experiences and perspectives'.

Mindset and the workplace

As a leader, you are a role model and your mindset and attitude play a significant role in how your staff also approach their day, and their willingness and ability to do a task. If you have an 'I get to' and a 'can do' attitude, chances are that attitude is going to rub off on those around you. Just like a good belly laugh, it's contagious.

Adopting a healthy mindset in the workplace creates a culture of continuous improvement (or kaizen, refer to chapter 3), resilience and innovation, and better staff retention because people want to work with positive people.

Here are a few ways to role-model a positive mindset for your team:

- *Encourage innovation:* Let creativity out of the cage — we all need to feel like we are growing.

- *Embrace challenges:* When solving problems, use the phrase 'we get to'.

- *Turn setbacks into learning and growth opportunities:* Don't brush over setbacks, but rather reflect on how you and your team can 'do better' next time.

- *Put time and energy into making your staff grow:* Don't train them as if your staff will only be with you for a short time; train them to be there for a lifetime.

- *Create a positive culture:* No-one wants to spend half of their waking life being miserable.

TAKING ACTION

Attitude really is a choice, and that choice is yours. The more charged your battery, the better your mental health and attitude will become. I make sure that I set myself up well for each day with my morning rhythm. I take care of my mental, emotional, physical wellbeing at the start of my day so I can set my sails for a positive day.

MINDSET TIPS

- Learn how to stop, connect and breathe — the tools in part III will help.
- Have an attitude of gratitude.
- Be kind to yourself and others.
- Focus on one habit you wish to change, and work through it.
- Move your body (to release the happy chemicals).
- Ask yourself each day, 'How can I be of service to others?'

TIME FOR ACTION QUESTIONS

- What's one limiting belief you have that's stopping you from being the best version of yourself?
- How does this impact you and the people around?
- What could you do to turn this limiting belief around to improve in this area of your life?

Hint: Unless you're perfect, you will find something!

LET'S MAKE IT HAPPEN!

Take one minute to set an intention to do one thing today or this week to improve your mindset.

TESTIMONIAL: DISCOVERING THE POWER OF THE CARDS

One of the worst aspects of depression for me is the sense of being trapped within its dark caverns, fearing there is no way out — or, worse, knowing there could be a way out if only there was a map.

I had just spent three weeks in one of those dark caves, just waiting for a glimpse of light to follow. Trapped inside, I experienced confused thinking, muddled thinking, a terrible fatigue and sense of hopelessness. All the advice I've heard about dealing with depression floods into my head — exercise, talk to somebody, self-nurture, blah, blah, blah. Instructions are fired like bullets and it's all so confusing, so damn hard, and my body is near to paralysed anyway. The only thing I can do is try to escape into sleep; to get unconscious.

I was just coming out of this three-week period of lying-on-the-bed-depression when a friend introduced me to this card system one morning. I can't remember the spread of the cards or all the simple instructions they offered me for the day, but I remember one in particular. It said, 'Decide what you want the next hour to look like'. It didn't suggest I plan the rest of my life or the year or even the next 24 hours — simply the next hour. I didn't know how I wanted the next hour to look but I did know I didn't want it to look like most of the hours in the previous three weeks. So I knew *not* to go and lie on the bed. As it happened, the vacuum cleaner was out, and I turned it on. That day I cleaned the house — which was in need of attention, and which was contributing to my depression. The decision not to lie down and try to escape, the action of cleaning and the outcome of a clean house completely changed my day. It changed the following days as well — I had been given a map with which to escape the hellish cavern that had been keeping me from my own life.

Having been shown how the cards work, I believe they are the most practical, simple and helpful tool for dealing with depression that I have ever encountered. I can see they are designed to help everyone who is dissatisfied with some area or areas of their lives, and are not just a tool for depression.

Congratulations to the designer of this system. I believe you have come up with something truly wonderful.

Sally

Chapter 8

Fun

It was one of those perfect summer days in Kingscliff, northern New South Wales. Not a cloud in the sky, the water was crystal clear, and the town was abuzz with locals and holiday-makers making the most of it. Over to my right, people were sprawled out on their towels and beach chairs on the riverbank, looking down onto the water where swimmers were doing laps, paddle boarders floated aimlessly, and families were soaking up the sun rays above and the salt water below. In front, a squadron of pelicans waited for their free feed of fish from the boaties who had just come in with their catch for the day, while the seagulls milled about like fans at a rock concert looking up at their heroes.

I scanned the picturesque scene that was laid out in front of me from right to left, breathing in the salt air and feeling the light breeze on my skin. Then my scan stopped abruptly at a glitch in the system. Standing about five metres to my left was a man dressed in shiny shoes, trousers and button-up shirt, cleanly shaven with his hair prim. He was longingly looking out at the playful scene taunting him with its beauty.

I realised he was also looking across at me, another man dressed in shiny shoes, trousers and button-up shirt, cleanly shaven with his hair prim and proper. 'Shaun', I said.

'Tim', he said. We closed the gap between us.

'Are you going for a swim?'

'Can't, got a meeting in 30 minutes. You?' he replied.

'Can't', I said, 'got a meeting in 30 minutes.'

We looked back out at the water glistening in the sunlight, two blokes living in paradise but having to enjoy it from the sidelines.

Redefining what success looks like

Standing on the riverbank that day, Shaun and I discussed the corner we seemed to have backed ourselves into — seeing it as a badge of honour to work hard around the clock to support our families and lifestyles, a sense of guilt hovering above our shoulders reminding us of our responsibilities, our adulthood, and that playing and having fun is reserved for the weekends and holidays.

We both turned on our heels and left paradise behind, making our way to meet another man dressed in shiny shoes, trousers and button-up shirt, cleanly shaven with his hair prim and proper. I realised I had gotten caught up in an expectation that wasn't mine, an expectation that life had to look a certain way and that if you were to be successful, you had to dress this way and you needed to act and talk that way. I have never been one to conform and follow, so how did I get stuck in a mould that didn't fit or feel comfortable for me? I needed to change what my picture of success looked like, rather than simply rely on one I had read in a book or listened to in a podcast. I had to move away from the clichés that demand you have to be the hardest working person in the room to be successful, that you've got to put in the hours and do the grind, sleep when you are dead, blah, blah, blah.

I realised I needed to step back and redefine what success looked like for me. When I stripped it all back and reconnected to my own inner thoughts and feelings, what success looked like was very simple. I wanted to be healthy, happy and a good person doing good things. I realised that fun had a key role to play in that success — because the more fun I had, the easier those other things came to fruition.

From that moment on, I vowed to keep a 'fun bag' in my car with my swimmers, towel, mask and snorkel and a few other things that meant, when I found myself with some time between meetings or felt like I needed a recharge, I was ready to go. I'd already discovered how beneficial siestas are for the mind and body, so of course I threw in a hammock as well.

I also started to research the benefits of play and how play can make you more creative and productive, improve brain function, relieve stress and keep you feeling youthful.[24] Innately, I knew these things, but responsibilities had combined to bury the importance of them. The tagline for my company Watersports Guru was 'Discover the fun' and our team building company's tagline was 'Teams that play together stay together' — yet, here I was trying to be Mr Serious because I was living from an expectation that wasn't even mine.

I had devoted my whole life to play, but had become busy being busy and forgotten what makes my heart sing. I'd become boring — and I hate being boring!

Since I packed that fun bag and put it in the car, I now make a deliberate effort to find the fun in each day—whether it's the little fun or the big fun—because I know it makes me a better person.

Finding your fun

Fun is my favourite wellness area, but it's also the one that we can pay the least attention to. You may think nothing is serious about having fun; however, did you know that having fun is one of the best things you can do to improve your mental health?

Fun invites you to create more space for life to be enjoyed, with moments that make you laugh, smile and play. Fun is finding ways to make the ordinary things extraordinary, and simply enjoying the surroundings you are in.

Fun is different for everyone. What I find fun might be different to what you find fun. In general, however, you can have two types of fun: I call them 'little fun' and 'big fun'.

'Little fun' is the easily accessible things that you can do every day—such as have a laugh, play games and banter. The little things you do each day to have fun can have a big impact on your mental health. I love to go for a beach walk each day with my family—for me, that's the little fun.

'Big fun' takes a bit more effort to make happen, and includes things you might get to do on a weekend, holiday or day off. For me, big fun is going for a surf, snorkel, hike or camping trip. Even though the little fun keeps my battery steady, the big fun is what boosts it.

I try to include other wellness areas into my fun — such as physical health (chapter 3), friendships (chapter 9) and relationships (chapter 11).

No doubt you know that when you have fun, you feel good, and it gives you warmth in your heart. However, did you know that fun boosts the production of happy chemicals in our brain?[25] The neurochemicals dopamine and serotonin get released when you're having fun, and this lifts your mood. It is extremely hard to feel sad or depressed when you're having fun.

Give yourself permission to have fun. For many years, I felt guilty when I wanted to take some time off to enjoy myself, especially while my staff were working. However, when I do take a break to have fun, I know that I become a much better version of myself and can be more present and giving to others.

Since 2017 at GreenX7, we have been measuring the wellbeing of individuals, teams and organisations, and one thing has become abundantly clear: we have forgotten how to have fun through play. While measuring the decline in play, the data was also pointing to an alarming rise of loneliness, chronic disease, vitamin D deficiency, depression and suicide. Overall, our data highlighted the growing trend of people spending more time indoors by themselves, spectating on screens, and less time outdoors participating in life with others.

What if we redefined play as a way of life, and not just something we do if we have some scrap of time left over? Here's how I now define play: **p**urposeful **l**eisure **a**ctivating **y**outhfulness. Because when you really look at the ingredients that make up play, you also start to understand how powerful it can be in preventing loneliness, chronic disease, depression and boredom.

Here are some further positive effects play can have on your wellbeing:

- boosting brain function and creativity

- reducing stress and enhances mental wellbeing

- improving social connections and relationships

- supporting emotional resilience and mental agility

- enhancing physical health and energy levels

- keeping you feeling youthful and engaged in life.

Have I convinced you to also always have a fun bag on hand?

Having fun at work and with your team

We also need to take a serious look at how we include fun into our culture at work, and one of the best ways to do this is through looking at Dr Mihaly Csikszentmihalyi's work on flow, which describes a psychological state of deep focus, immersion and enjoyment in an activity. This state occurs when skill level and challenge are balanced, leading to enhanced performance, creativity and intrinsic motivation. Being a state of flow is linked to greater wellbeing and peak human experiences, often found in sports, arts and work. As Dr Csikszentmihalyi noted, 'Play is flow in its purest form — we become completely absorbed in the moment, lose track of time, and perform at our peak'.[26]

Flow and play interlink in the following ways at work:

- encouraging creativity and innovation

- improving intrinsic motivation and productivity

- reducing stress and increasing wellbeing
- promoting collaboration and engagement.[27]

Consider the following ways to integrate play into your and your teams' workday:

- Introduce short, playful energiser activities during breaks — for example, 'thumb wars'.
- Foster creativity with hands-on, playful brainstorming sessions.
- Encourage team challenges and friendly competitions.
- Allow for flexible work setups that include playful furniture or activity zones.
- Integrate nature-based activities into the workday.
- Organise themed workdays or spontaneous fun activities.
- Encourage social connection through collaborative, playful experiences.
- Create a company culture that values lightheartedness and fun in daily tasks.
- Allow time for unstructured play and creative thinking.

TAKING ACTION

Don't feel guilty about having fun. You deserve to let your hair down — life is for living! Your team will also thank you for it.

FUN TIPS

- Have a fun bag ready to go.
- Phone a friend or get your family involved.

(continued)

- Schedule a fun hour with your team each week — for example, frisbee in the park.

- Write a 'play' list covering activities you can do in 30 minutes, 1 hour, 2 hours, half a day or a full day, and stick it to your fridge — so when you have that time, it's not wasted binge eating or binge watching, and being a spectator.

TIME FOR ACTION QUESTIONS

- What do you like to do for fun?

- When was the last time you had fun?

- How does your battery feel when you are having fun?

- How does your battery feel when you haven't had fun for a while?

LET'S MAKE IT HAPPEN!

Take one minute to set an intention to do one 'little fun' thing today and one 'big fun' activity for this week. Put it in your diary, phone a friend and lock it in! Recharge your battery.

Chapter 9
Friendships

The other night we had our friend Innes over for dinner, which is a rarity for me because, honestly, you don't normally get two words out of me after dark. I'm an early bird and very much an extrovert in the morning, but once evening comes around, you would have more luck having an engaging conversation with a plant. But there are some people who, no matter what time of day or night, no matter what state your house or your brain is in, your door is always open to — and Innes is one such person for us. Over a very wholesome Buddha bowl, I asked her if she had watched any good series lately — we had just finished *Homeland* and were in need of another series to 'veg out' to at night when the kids go down.

Without hesitation, Innes suggested *Grey's Anatomy*, which I had never watched (although I had to admit I had heard about 'McDreamy'). Now, that precious time slot at night cannot be wasted on just any series — it has to be good. So I asked her to give me her reasons why, above all others, this was the series to watch. Innes imparted her wisdom, explained that she just loves the friendship dynamic between Meredith and Cristina and how, no matter what happens, they continue to be besties throughout. She said it was like they had both 'found their people', and she loved watching them together.

This led to a wonderful discussion about just what 'finding your people' means — who are they, and why. We decided they are the people in your life that share your qualities and values, who you never get sick of, and can tell them anything. A connection that is just there and you don't have to work at it. You know — 'your people'. Whether you've known them for a lifetime or maybe just a short while, the saying 'you know when you know' just seems to apply.

Fighting loneliness — one friendship at a time

If you are reading this and do feel lonely, wondering where 'your people' are, you are certainly not alone. I'm afraid that as a society we seem to be struggling to find 'our people'. Loneliness has become more than just a social issue; it is a growing public health crisis with profound psychological, physiological and societal impacts. So much so, it is now referred to as the 'loneliness epidemic'. In fact, loneliness costs the Australian economy approximately $2.7 billion per year in health-related expenses.[28]

Let's take a deep dive into what loneliness is, including its impacts and how you can support yourself and help others if you found yourself in this situation — because, looking at the stats, if it's not you who is lonely, chances are it's someone around you.

Loneliness is a subjective emotional state in which a person feels socially isolated, even if they are surrounded by others, which means that even if you're living with someone you can still feel lonely.

The four types of loneliness are as follows:

- *Emotional loneliness:* A lack of deep, meaningful relationships or emotional closeness with others.

- *Social loneliness:* The absence of a wider social network or group interactions.

- *Situational loneliness:* Temporary loneliness due to life transitions, such as moving to a new city or starting a new job.

- *Chronic loneliness:* A persistent feeling of loneliness lasting for weeks, months or even years, which can impact physical and mental health.

When I started to research the impacts loneliness had on our wellbeing, I was shocked at the significant health effects, including an increased risk of depression and anxiety, higher stress levels and weakened immune function, and a greater likelihood of heart disease, stroke and high blood pressure. Additionally, loneliness has been linked to cognitive decline and a higher risk of dementia in older adults.[29] The one stat that really got me was that loneliness has been linked to serious mental and physical health consequences, often compared to smoking 15 cigarettes per day,[30] — so please don't be a lonely smoker!

How we got to having a loneliness epidemic in the developed world is multifaceted, with links back to the Industrial Revolution — prior to which, for example only 1 in 100 people lived alone compared to 1 in 7 now living alone. However, as

I mentioned, even if you are living with others, you can still feel lonely — and this is where technology has had the biggest impact.

Let's look at just one way technology has increased loneliness — what has become known as 'phubbing', or snubbing someone in favour of your phone. I'm sure we've all been guilty of this at some time, choosing scrolling through your phone over the intimacy of a face-to-face conversation. Unsurprisingly, this has been linked to decreased relationship satisfaction and increased feelings of isolation.

I'm sure you see it all the time or feel it — whether it's at work while trying to have a conversation, at the cafe drinking coffee or on the couch at home, there always seems to be phubbing going on. Now, this is not an easy problem to solve because the dopamine hit we are getting from our phones is what's causing our attention to stray. But it is possible!

Try the following to help you from phubbing:

- Set phone-free zones and times by designating areas such as the dining table, bedroom or social gatherings as phone-free spaces. Establish specific 'no phone' times, such as during meals, conversations or date nights.

- Use the 'phone stack' game when out with friends or family by having everyone stack their phones face down on the table. The first person who grabs their phone pays for coffee or does a fun challenge.

- Turn off non-essential notifications by disabling alerts for social media, emails and non-urgent apps to reduce distractions. Set your phone to 'do not disturb' during conversations.

- Keep your phone out of reach by placing it in another room or in a bag when socialising to resist the urge to check it. Use a watch instead of your phone to check the time to avoid distractions.

- Use the 80/20 rule for phone use by spending 80 per cent of your time engaging with real-life interactions and only 20 per cent checking your phone when necessary. Be mindful of the 'one-screen rule' by focusing on one thing at a time instead of multitasking with your phone.

- Practise active listening by putting your phone down, maintaining eye contact, and fully engaging in conversations. Show you're listening by nodding, responding and asking follow-up questions.

- Use apps such as Forest, Moment or Apple's screen time tool to track and reduce phone usage. Set daily screen time goals to be more mindful of in-person interactions.

- Lead by example if you want others to stop phubbing by modelling the behaviour first. Express to friends and family why you're prioritising presence over screens.

- Replace scrolling with real conversations by starting a conversation instead of checking your phone. Suggest fun activities such as games, walks or storytelling to keep interactions engaging.

- Set a social agreement by having an open discussion with friends, family or co-workers about limiting phone use during quality time. Encourage a culture where being fully present is valued and respected.

Being a friend to make a friend

I love the quote from Ralph Waldo Emerson that 'The only way to have a friend is to be one'. This reminds us to reflect on ourselves and if we truly are a good friend. No doubt you have your own opinion on what makes a good friend, which might differ from mine, but I'm also guessing some traits apply to most.

Friends are those people with whom you share a genuine connection or bond; the people who show up when you need them most. What's important is not how many friends we have but how many friends we can count on to be honest, open and there when we need them — rather than just take the best Instagram photo.

Humans are inherently social creatures. We all need connection; the chance to spend time with others, to feel seen and understood, and to know that someone will be there when we need them. These moments of connection do more than comfort us emotionally. They activate powerful neurochemicals like oxytocin, dopamine and serotonin, which help us feel safe, uplifted and motivated. But beyond the chemistry, true friendships foster something even deeper. They nurture the three essential ingredients I introduced in chapter 1 that help us build self-worth: value, meaning and belonging.

Certain friends give you energy, while others may steal it away. Now might be a suitable time to reflect on this, and think about the type of friends you have or the type of friend you are — and how you might attract more good friends into your life. On this subject, let me give you a personal example.

Last week I was playing with my kids at our local pirate ship park, and another dad was there with a boy a similar age to Frankie. When our eyes met from across the slide, we both did the head nod with a smile. Now, here's the sliding door moment.

Option 1: I could ignore the other dad and put all my attention onto my kids. (Fair play, an understandable choice, and no-one will judge.)

Option 2: After the head nod and smile, I could start a conversation.

'G'day mate, I'm Tim.'

'Nick. How you going?'

'Good. Do you live locally? I haven't seen you here before.'

'We just moved up from Sydney last month, and living around the corner.'

'How are you finding the area?' I could ask.

'It's a great spot, but we're just trying to find our feet as we don't really know anyone up here.'

This creates another sliding door moment.

Option 1: I could sum up the person and decide, 'nice enough but probably not my person'. And I could go back to putting all my focus on the kids.

Option 2: I could decide I liked this person, and that he could be a possible future friend. From here, I could converse some more — asking, for example, what Nick did for work and for fun.

No doubt you've worked out I took option 2 at both 'sliding door' moments. Nick and I ended up talking about all sorts of stuff, including how AI could possibly affect his job as a YouTube agent (think sports agent but for YouTube influencers), and other epic kid's playgrounds in the area. We added each other on Instagram and made a few comments later to just reconfirm that 'hey, you're a guy who I see value from hanging out with'.

And, just like that, I've made a potential friend.

You might be thinking, *That's all great, but what if I don't have kids and a pirate ship park around the corner? How can I meet a potential friend?* Glad you asked.

The potential meeting places for friends are many, so first think about what you like to do. What interests do you currently have or what new interests would you like to adopt? If I wanted to become a runner, for example, I'd look at joining the 'parkrun' in my area and hopefully meet my new running buddy. If I've just moved to a coastal town with kids over five years old, I could look at joining the local surf club. If you're a creative night owl, you could consider going to a 'paint and sip' event, and if you're a book worm, you could join a local book club. I've even had a friend borrow my labrador, Sailor, to take to dog parks and walks along the beach (although I'm pretty sure that was to find a potential life partner). And don't forget your workplace — you already know you've got a least one thing in common with your work mates.

All of these scenarios require one thing from you — to put yourself out there and giving it a go, which means no longer hiding behind your phone! You have to stop living indoors spectating, step outside and go participate in your life. Yes, it might be uncomfortable and, yes, you might face some rejection, but on the other side of that might be waiting 'your person' — and a friendship as beautiful and solid as the dynamic between Meredith and Cristina on *Grey's Anatomy*, Chandler and Joey on *Friends*, Will and Grace (on the show of the same name), and even Winnie the Pooh and Piglet.

Building friendships at work

Before having a family, I seemed to have plenty of time to hang out with my mates outside of work and on the weekends. Now

I have kids, my purpose of making sure I'm being an awesome father and husband inevitably means I need to put the time in to create the connection with my closest relationships — which, of course, doesn't leave me much time for friendships.

I've been able to combat this through creating friendships at work. You've probably heard the saying, 'It can be lonely at the top'. And if you're in any kind of leadership role, you know it holds some truth. You're the one making the big calls, holding space for the team and keeping the energy up — often without anyone asking how you're doing. You can feel like you need to maintain a bit of distance just to keep things running. But here's the thing: we're not wired to do life — or leadership — alone. One of the biggest game changers for sustainable energy at work is having genuine friendships and real conversations. You need people you can laugh with, vent to or just share a coffee with in silence. When you start building those kinds of connections at work, especially as a leader, the load gets lighter. Your job is still to lead — but now you're not doing it on an island. You're surrounded by humans, not just roles. This doesn't mean you have to blurt out all your insecurities and concerns to those willing to listen; however, it is okay to connect with those around you at a deeper level.

Here are some ways to build genuine connections at work:

- Know that you don't have to be friends with everyone (but you do have to be kind to everyone). Even a couple of good work mates will recharge your battery.

- Integrate work and play together — go for a walking meeting or run, hit the gym or play a racquet sport.

- Find someone who enjoys the same hobby as you and use this as a brain break.

All of these will help re-engage the brain for the afternoon and keep your body maintained.

I've seen the benefits of this approach in my own life. As I touched on in chapter 5, I'm not 'ripped' and I've never really been a 'gym guy'. I've always preferred being outdoors — that's where I come alive. But now, in my 40s, I'm feeling the shift. Staying physically strong takes more effort, but I know myself well enough to admit that hitting the gym solo just doesn't do it for me.

That's where Jace comes in. After 17 years of military service, over a decade of which was with the elite Australian Special Forces, he's now navigating the transition into civilian life. We've been working together on a new GreenX7 connected leadership program, and instead of meeting in an office or over coffee, we've made the local gym our meet-up spot. While we train, we chat, plan and bounce ideas. Apparently I need to build a resilient body in my old age just as much as a I need to build a resilient mind.

It's the perfect blend of work and friendship — we're making progress on a project we both care about, forming a real connection, and getting a good physical workout. I'm not just ticking a box on health; I'm getting stronger, building a meaningful friendship, and making work feel more human.

TAKING ACTION

At the end of the day, you know it's the real-life connections that matter rather than those lived through a screen — so get out there and make some.

FRIENDSHIP TIPS

- Be real and honest.
- Ensure your friendships are based on respect and trust.

- Make time for your friends.

- Be present and actively listen.

- Give and don't just take.

- Be there through the ups and downs.

- Be someone who gives energy to others.

TIME FOR ACTION QUESTIONS

- How are your friendships at the moment?

- What does it mean to be a good friend?

- Are you a good friend?

- Who do you need to reconnect with?

- Where could you possibly find your next friend?

LET'S MAKE IT HAPPEN!

Take one minute to set an intention to do one thing today or this week to improve one of your friendships. Put it in your diary, phone a friend and lock it in! Recharge your battery.

CASE STUDY: BILL'S LONELINESS JOURNEY

On paper, Bill's life looked solid. He was living in inner-city Brisbane with his wife of 28 years, was a hands-on father to three adult kids, ran his own business, and had a decent social rhythm—including basketball with mates, a shared office with friendly faces, and regular catch-ups with friends. But something was missing.

Despite all the external activity, Bill felt deeply lonely. The move to a new suburb had disconnected him from his favourite coffee shop crew, his gym community, and a volunteer group he loved. The sense of belonging he once had was gone—and he felt it. Counselling helped him realise he'd been living as a 'people pleaser', putting everyone else first and, in the process, losing touch with who he was.

Eventually, Bill made one of the hardest decisions of his life—he left his marriage. Although the relationship had many good memories, it had become one where he no longer felt heard, valued or free to be himself. The emotional toll of trying to maintain peace at the expense of his own wellbeing had caught up with him. Ending the relationship was painful but necessary.

Needing space to heal, Bill left Brisbane altogether and relocated solo to a small coastal town, hoping the ocean, sunsets and slower pace would help him breathe again—literally and emotionally. It was a risky decision for someone already feeling isolated, but the city had begun to feel suffocating.

In his new town, he did what he knew: kept moving, kept working, kept showing up. He joined a local gym, swam daily—even in winter—and travelled back to Brisbane to keep playing basketball. But he was still running on empty.

Everything began to shift with a few connections. A chance encounter with an old friend at a local restaurant and, later, a few regulars at the beach, cracked open the door to community. After Bill started swimming with a small group, he took initiative and created a WhatsApp thread—adding everyone under the shared last name 'Swims'.

What started as a few casual dips turned into a thriving community of over 40 people. They swim together every morning, all year round, followed by a standing coffee ritual. That swim group became Bill's anchor—not just for physical wellness, but also for daily social connection and emotional grounding.

Along the way, Bill also found himself cautiously entering a new relationship—this time with stronger boundaries, clearer needs and a deeper understanding of himself. After 20 intentional dates, hours of phone chats and plenty of real conversation, he found what he calls 'grade nine vibes'—playful, respectful and calm.

Bill's story is a reminder that the cure for loneliness isn't one big fix. It's many small, intentional choices. It's showing up. It's creating space for conversation, friendship, movement and joy. And, sometimes, it means walking away from what no longer serves you—so you can finally reconnect with what does.

Chapter 10

Relationships

The word 'relationships' seems to bring up a whole mixed bag of feelings for so many different reasons. Sometimes just uttering this word in a coaching session will cause clients to cry or beam with happiness. Other times, I can feel a person's whole body shut down in front of my eyes. One thing for certain is that relationships have a massive impact on our lives — both positive and negative.

I remember in my early 20s I felt so hurt by humanity that I focused all of my limited emotional aptitude on the conservation of sea animals — because I felt that humans didn't deserve to be helped. My outlet at the time was boxing, and I felt so much pain and anger towards certain characters who had come in and out of my life that every time I stepped into the boxing ring, I would picture their head on my opponents, and that anger fuelled me through the rounds.

I associated relationships with pain because I didn't have the emotional intelligence back then to understand that humans are a complicated species with many facets at play.

I lost many good relationships throughout my 20s because I didn't understand what a relationship needed to thrive. Instead, I allowed these relationships to whittle away and fade out to oblivion, but still somehow ended up with an emotional anchor to carry into the next one.

By the time I reached my late 20s, I had built a fortress around my heart, so it was kept safe from fear and pain. I still enjoyed companionship and love, but what I know now of love is vastly different to how I perceived it back then.

After many years of chipping away at the walls that I built up and allowing myself to forgive, I gave myself the opportunity to feel warmth and trust with others. Little by little, I allowed another person to delicately hold my heart.

Today, over a decade later, I'm filled with love and joy that I'm able to reciprocate to others — stark contrast to how I used to be. I now find it so refreshing to seek out the positives in each interaction I have with each individual I meet, rather than judging from a distance.

Building and nurturing positive relationships

I have no idea of your own current situation. Each of us is at a different stage in our life. You might be single and living your best life, or you might be on the verge of a divorce and feel like you have nothing else to give. Or perhaps you are just starting what could be your life's greatest love affair. Whatever your current situation, I think we can all agree that love and relationships can have an overwhelming impact on our lives.

So many of my views and opinions have changed this past decade when I reflect on my own relationships. After spending years working on becoming a better human, and knowing that I have a deep love and respect for myself for doing the work, I now see the pay-off for me and those around me. I have so much love, respect, trust and affection for my amazing wife, Carly. I now have the tools to continue to thrive, and not just survive, in our marriage and now with our kids, who fill my heart with so much joy. I know that if I had become a dad 10 years ago, I wouldn't have had the capacity to reciprocate this incredible love from my family.

And I've learned how to forgive those who caused me so much pain in the past. I no longer need to step into a ring and box out my anger. I can sit and breathe out any frustrations. I'm far from being a saint, but I've come a long way.

Relationships help you explore those deeper, more intimate connections you have with those you care about. Whether the relationship is with yourself, or your partner, kids, family or friends, the warmth of that relationship can give us the greatest joy in our lives.

When you make the time to deepen your connection with those who are closest to you and make them feel valued, you create strong, healthy relationships.

Positive relationships help create trust, and build deeper and more meaningful emotions. They also provide companionship and a sense of belonging, which gives us value. And the quality of our relationships can increase our resilience, an important element in combating the daily stresses of life.

A thriving relationship is built on connection, trust, respect and making the other person feel valued. It's about creating a sense of meaning and belonging. But like anything worth having, you've got to keep showing up for it. You can't get lazy and expect it to take care of itself. Relationships need daily attention. Think of them like an investment. The more consistent the effort, the better the return. Relationship expert John Gottman talks about the five-to-one ratio — five positive interactions for every one negative. That's what helps hold things together when life gets messy, when you're stressed, snappy or just not your best. It's those small, daily acts of care that build the kind of trust that stays solid even when everything else feels like it's falling apart.

Some of the ways Carly and I nurture our relationship include the following:

- *Switching off technology at mealtimes:* Every time we eat breakfast, lunch or dinner together, we make sure that all technology is switched off and we are 100 per cent present with each other.

- *Greeting each other with love:* We also make a conscious effort to welcome each other with love each time we come through the door. We want each other to feel excited about coming home rather than dreading what they will find on the other side. We turn off the TV, close the laptop, stop cooking or whatever else we are doing to make sure that we meet and greet each other at the door. We make a big deal of it, saying something like, 'Hey babe, welcome home. How's your day been?' This way, we know we each get a positive feeling every time we come home.

- *Having quality connection time each day:* Finally, we make a conscious effort to include each other in our daily rhythm so that we can spend quality time together in nature. For us, that is going to the beach or park each morning while watching the kids zoom about.

Supporting each other's wellbeing

When you're in a deep relationship with someone, inevitably you are going to argue or have disagreements. Some of these disagreements may be about the silliest things. Sometimes, and especially when your battery is low and you're under stress, these disagreements can feel insurmountable. For me, in those moments, if I have the presence of mind, I ask myself, 'Is this disagreement worth affecting the wellbeing of myself and Carly'?

My role in our marriage is to support Carly's wellbeing, and she does the same for me. We are there to nurture and look out for one another, as a team. If I can see her battery is getting low, I'll let her do what she needs to recharge — and vice versa. Sometimes, you are the one who sees what your partner needs before they do and I believe it's your responsibility to speak up, and allow them the space and time to nurture themselves.

And if you're both in survival mode at the same time? You must make time to reconnect and find out how best to support each other's wellbeing. Unfortunately, this is another one of those sliding door moments (similar to what I talk about with friendships in the previous chapter), and your choices in these moments can either create a deeper connection or push a wedge between you. Most of us have a tendency to shut down and go inwards when in survival mode, pushing that person away yet again. This was a cycle I was stuck in for many years — get hurt, push away. What I had to realise was that this person wasn't intentionally trying to hurt me. Of course, if they are, that's certainly not a relationship you want to stay in. However, in the case where two people genuinely love and care for each other, the situational circumstance is what is often coming between you. If this is the case, you need to take the time and consciously choose to make a change, so you can both move forward in a positive direction.

Let me give you an example of consciously choosing to move forward together in my relationship with Carly. Most mornings, I try to wake up at around 4.30 or 5 am (depending on the kids the night before). I do my morning stretches, have my coffee while reading, and then get stuck into what I call my 'hour of power' — that is, my deepest work at the time. (Right now, it's writing this book.) At 6.45 am, I go inside to where Carly has been dealing with the kids for the last hour or two. Now, at this stage, I would love nothing more than to grab my board and go for a surf, but I know that Carly also needs to recharge her battery, so we tag-in and she either takes Hugo for a walk or goes for a run, sometimes meeting me and the kids at the beach. This routine is constantly changing, depending on the ebbs and flows of parenting, but we always make sure we let each other recharge each day. Why? Because we are better partners and parents when we do.

Building positive relationships at work

Depending on your work situation, you might find yourself spending more time with your colleagues than with your own family. That's why it's so important to nurture those relationships, and build something positive, supportive and human. It's no surprise so many organisations refer to their teams as 'family' — and it's more than just a feel-good phrase. The word *culture* actually comes from the Latin word *cultus*, which means *to care for, to cultivate.*

In essence, your workplace culture is the result of what you tend to — including how you support each other, communicate and show up day to day. A thriving culture isn't built on policies or posters — it's built on care. When people feel seen, supported and part of something meaningful, culture becomes more than a buzzword. It becomes a feeling. A rhythm. A lived experience. As a leader, it's up to you to foster this care, and to attract the right people who will help support this — and not hinder all your hard work.

I mention in the previous chapter the saying, 'It can be lonely at the top' — but I didn't say 'is'. Many successful working relationships have thrived and, due to this, so have their organisations.

Here are some examples of successful working relationships:

- *Steve Jobs and Steve Wozniak:* The co-founders of Apple, where Jobs was the visionary and Wozniak the engineering genius.

- *Sergey Brin and Larry Page:* Co-founders of Google who transformed the way we find and use information.

- *Warren Buffett and Charlie Munger:* Legendary investing partners at Berkshire Hathaway.

- *Ben Cohen and Jerry Greenfield:* Founders of Ben & Jerry's who brought social values into business.

- *Phil Jackson and Michael Jordan:* A coach/player dynamic that helped create a basketball dynasty.

- *Oprah Winfrey and Gayle King:* Lifelong friends and professional collaborators.

These duos were more than just great friendships — they were built on real trust, shared goals and the kind of connection that grows through the highs and the hard times. What made them work wasn't that things were always easy, but that both people kept showing up. They put in the effort, stayed in the conversation and kept moving forward — together. What set them apart wasn't perfection, but persistence — a shared commitment to the bigger picture, and a willingness to do the work that lasting success demands. That's the kind of relationship that doesn't just survive — it thrives.

So how can you cultivate these kinds of relationships in your workplace? How do you, as a leader, find that person who becomes your other half of the duo — the one who balances you, challenges you, and helps carry the load?

It starts with being *human first, leader second*. Let go of the idea that leadership is about having all the answers. Instead, create space for curiosity, vulnerability and shared wins. Look for the people who aren't just skilled, but also care deeply — about the mission, the people and the impact. You're looking for the ones who lean in when things get hard, who ask the tough questions and hold you accountable with heart.

You don't *assign* these relationships — you build them, slowly and intentionally, through honest conversations, shared challenges and showing up for each other when it counts.

Sometimes your other half shows up as the opposite of you — calm to your fire, detail to your big picture. Other times, they're a mirror, reflecting your best and calling out your blind spots. Either way, the magic lies in the mutual investment. Like any meaningful connection, a great working relationship isn't found, but instead, cultivated.

And when you find that person? Hold onto them. Because in a world that moves fast and often feels fragmented, that kind of partnership is not just powerful — it's rare.

To cultivate your 'other half' at work, try the following:

- *Lead with curiosity, not control:* Be open to different perspectives. Ask questions, listen deeply and create space for real dialogue.

- *Look beyond skills and focus on alignment:* Find people who share your values, not just your goals. Skills can be taught; shared purpose can't.

- *Invest in trust before task:* Relationships aren't built in meetings — they're built in moments. A chat over coffee can go further than a strategy session.

- *Be willing to show vulnerability:* Share the hard days, not just the wins. True connection comes from being real, not just being right.

- *Respect your differences:* Your best work often comes from tension, rather than sameness. Honour the contrast — it's part of the creative spark.

- *Communicate, even when it's uncomfortable:* Don't bury the friction. Lean into it with respect and honesty. This is how trust is strengthened.

- *Celebrate together and reflect together:* Acknowledge the journey, not just the destination. Reflecting on what you've navigated builds depth and loyalty.

- *Show up consistently:* Reliability is rare — and powerful. Be the person someone can count on, and you'll likely find the same in return.

TAKING ACTION

Building, and nurturing, a positive relationship takes time and effort — but the rewards in terms of deeper connection and support are well worth it.

RELATIONSHIP TIPS

- Remember — it's the little things each day that build trust and respect.

- Connect, don't just communicate.

- Allow each other time to pursue your own passions or have fun.

- Have fun together.

- Find out you and your partner's love language or work language.[31]

- Create a ritual together and stick to it.

TIME FOR ACTION QUESTIONS

- Who are the people in your life you have a deeper relationship with?

- How connected do you feel with these people right now?

- What could you do to improve the close relationships in your life?

LET'S MAKE IT HAPPEN!

Take one minute to set an intention to do one thing today or this week to connect with someone close to you and help them feel valued. Put it in your diary, phone a friend and lock it in! Recharge your battery.

Chapter 11

The wellness wheel

In the previous chapters in this part, I've outlined the eight wellness areas that make up your personal battery. Supporting each of these areas in your life not only keeps you healthy, happy and balanced, but is also a sure-fire way to build and maintain your resilience through the ups and downs of life.

Importantly, each wellness area is interconnected and, when combined, help support you in all facets of your day-to-day life. Typically, if you are lagging in a few areas, it can have a knock-on effect with the others. It also works the other way — the more areas you're on top of, the easier it becomes with the others.

For example, sleep can have a huge knock-on effect in many areas. I know, personally, if I have had a terrible nights sleep, I'll wake, and not have the motivation to do any sort of activity, which then affects my physical and mental health. I'll feel bad, so I'll comfort eat, which affects my nutrition. All those things accumulate to have a snowballing negative impact on my mental health. If I'm feeling down, I'm less likely to allow myself to have fun, which means I'm probably not catching up with my mates. This makes me feel like I'm not supporting my friends, which, of course, is going to rub off on my relationships. You can see how each of the areas can affect another. If your battery is low, it's extremely tough to put your best foot forward while trying to thrive each and every day.

To illustrate how each of the wellness areas interacts, I created the wellness wheel, shown in the following figure. The beauty of the wellness wheel is that you can use it to get a better picture of how you're travelling at this moment in your life, by shading in your rating for each element. At the centre of the wheel is 0 per cent. If you give yourself this rating for a particular area, you have some significant improvements to make. At the outer rim of the wheel sits 100 per cent — as you can likely guess, if you give yourself this rating, you're thriving in this area.

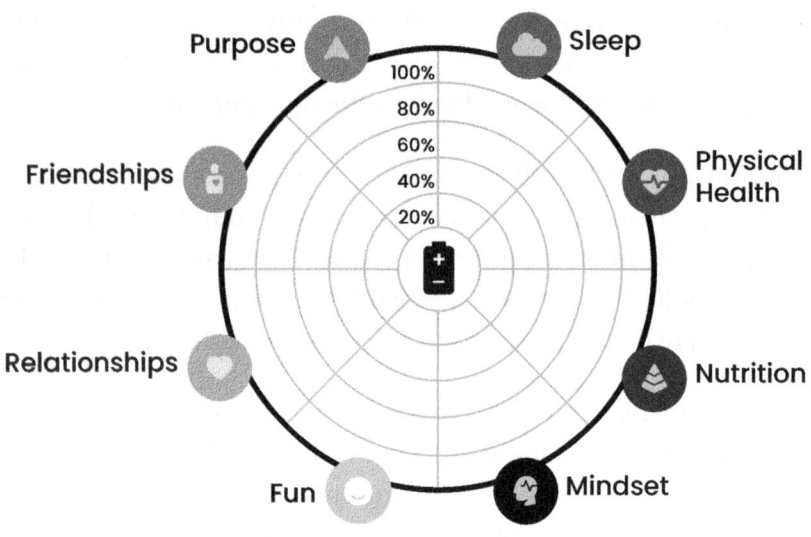

The wellness wheel

To gain a picture of your overall battery health, draw a line on each element where you feel you're sitting now, and then shade it in. Once you've completed all areas, you will have a better understanding of how you are travelling and what areas in your life you may need to focus on to pump up that wheel. Think of this as being similar to a bicycle wheel. Your tyre being full or flat will make a big difference on how hard you have to peddle to get through each day — especially if you hit lots of potholes!

TAKE A MOMENT

Before we head into the chapters in part III, let's take a moment to reconnect.

So many of us are so busy getting through our days and juggling all our balls that we think our 'to-do list' is the most important thing in our life. We get focused on tasks and forget about ourselves and our relationships. We live so much in our heads that we forget life is lived through our hearts.

Is a perfectly tidy house more important than having quality time with your family? Can the work emails wait until you have had a decent lunch break?

Is the purpose of your life to be a slave to society's commands, or is the Dalai Lama correct in saying 'The purpose of life is to be happy'?

If you prefer the Dalai Lama's take, I want you to take a moment and think about all the things that make you happy — the things that light you up and make your heart sing. How often are you doing these things?

We can all get so caught up with the wants of now and keeping busy that we are also constantly stuck in our heads, thinking that's what is important. We can too easily forget that all the good stuff happens through our heart space — including our fondest memories, our treasured moments and the things that when life ends will capture whether we endured or enjoyed. To get back to this heart space, we need to disconnect from the busyness and reconnect to self, others and nature.

RECONNECTING TO SELF

The first place to start is to reconnect with 'you'. I admit that it took me some time to understand what this meant. Put simply, it means to stop, think and feel where you are at right now in your life, and what you could do to improve and point your compass to your 'true north'. In simplicity, reflect on where you are and what you need to do to move forward in a positive direction.

Many of us rush through our day with constant distractions, especially technology.

Do you have any quiet time in your day to reflect on how you feel?

When's the last time you got bored and, instead of reaching for a screen to entertain yourself, used your imagination?

Reconnecting to self is about creating the time and space for you to think about you and what it is you need to reconnect and recharge.

My challenge for you is to, each day, find time to reconnect to you. Go for a walk, meditate, do some yoga, go for a surf, go for a bike ride, or even step into the garden for a few minutes — make it fun and it will get done!

You need to step away from noise on a constant basis to be able to ask yourself some important questions:

- How much energy do I have?
- Am I looking after my own wellbeing?
- Am I doing what makes me happy?

As the flight attendants remind us on the plane, we need to put on our own oxygen mask first before we can help others.

RECONNECTING TO OTHERS

In our modern world, we love our technology — whether it's a phone, tablet, computer, TV or smartwatches, some form of technology is not normally too far away. We are more connected than we have ever been before. We can connect instantly with family and friends around the world, and can see friends' holiday photos before they even get home. We can share news with our nearest and dearest instantly, and know everything about everyone the moment it has happened. Gone are the days when everyone would gather around the kitchen table while you flicked through photos narrating your holiday, reliving your best memories, while everyone murmured how lucky and adventurous you were.

We might appear to have lots of friends on social media, but how many true friends do we have in our lives that will support us through our dark times? We might share news on social media, but how often do we connect in person with those we care about anymore? When we do catch up with friends and family, are we truly present or are we distracted by our technology that sits on the table in front of us, commanding our attention.

Just because you're with someone, it doesn't mean that you're filling up their emotional cup — and vice versa. As a society, we have become so good at being physically present without being emotionally present that it's created a void of feeling valued and that we belong.

To have quality relationships, you need to be present, and you need to value the time you are sharing with that person in front of you. Again, you need to create the time and space for that relationship to thrive, and not just survive.

RECONNECTING TO NATURE

Nature is an amazing medicine cabinet that we have all around us and can use to enhance our wellbeing. I'm sure you've noticed how good you feel after spending time in the great outdoors. When I started looking into the science behind the benefits of our natural environment, it blew me away! Green space, water sources and sunshine are critical for our wellbeing, yet in our modern lives we are spending less and less time outdoors. We didn't evolve to spend all our time cooped up indoors in front of our screens.

We need to get outdoors to recharge our batteries. Personally, I love to paddleboard, surf, walk on the beach and snorkel to reconnect to nature. I always feel better after I do.

In nature, I can get away from the noise, marketing and hype of modern life, clear my mind and remind myself of what makes me genuinely happy. Sometimes, I like to just sit on the grass or beach in silence, reflecting on what is truly important and real for me. Other times, I'll string up a hammock and fall asleep because that is what I felt like doing. Doing nothing inspires creativity and helps me to come back to a path that is right for me — my true north.

These three processes of reconnecting to self, others and nature can keep you grounded, and keep you living a life from your own wants and needs, not influenced by everything around you. They can help you get out of your head and back into your heart — and so help you live and love again.

PART III

RECHARGING YOUR BATTERY WITH THE GREENX7 TOOLS

The GreenX7 tools are the foundation of a life well lived — the secret sauce, the magic formula for everyday wellness. These are the tools I rely on daily to stay grounded, to reconnect, and to create a rhythm that supports my mental, emotional, physical and spiritual health. They are not just concepts; they are the result of years of research, practice and real-world application — they have been tested, refined and proven to enhance wellbeing. And soon, you'll understand why.

As shown in the following figure, the GreenX7 tools are movement, environment, earthing, time, connection, breath and reflection. At their heart, these tools are designed to help you reconnect — to yourself, to others and to nature. Each tool serves a unique purpose, yet when combined, they create something far greater than the sum of their parts. They form a whole-systems approach to wellbeing that is both simple and sustainable, giving you a framework to build your own life rhythm — one that nurtures balance, energy and resilience.

In today's world, we are drifting further from these essential elements. With rising rates of loneliness, suicide, chronic disease and mental illness, modern society has shifted toward a sedentary, tech-driven and often disconnected way of living. We've deprioritised the very things that keep us healthy, happy and thriving.

This is where the GreenX7 tools come in. Each one has individual benefits, but it's when they work together that the real magic happens. And that's exactly what we're about to explore. Let's get into it, shall we?

The GreenX7 tools

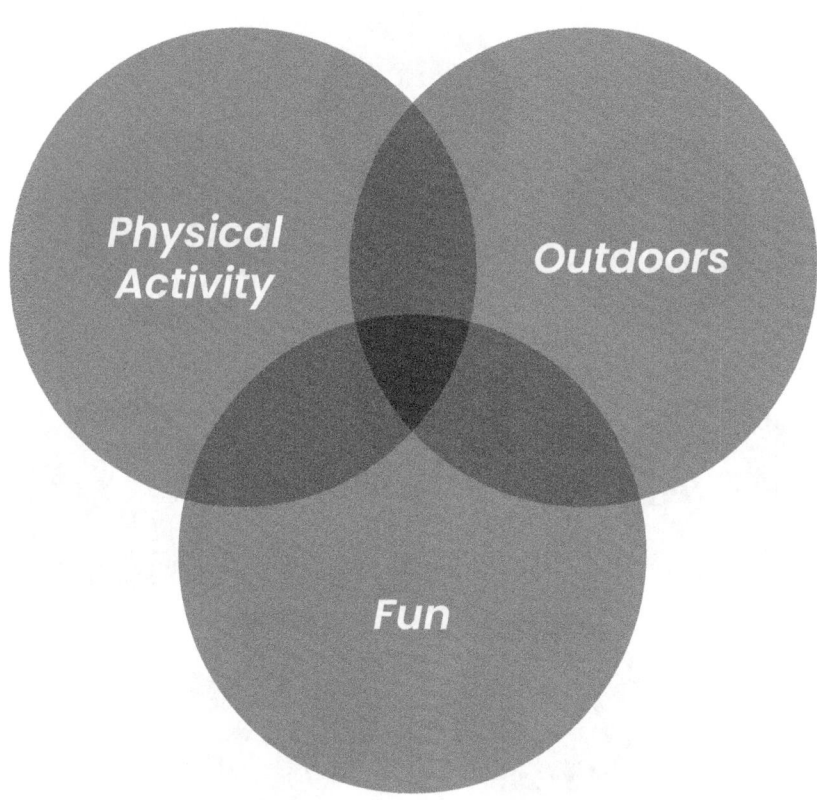

Elements of the movement GreenX7 tool

Chapter 12

Movement

Movement has always been a big part of my life. When I was growing up, I'm sure that I could have been diagnosed with ADHD and given some prescription to 'calm my farm'. Luckily for me, however, sports and nature were always just outside the front door, and those places celebrate high energy. (Just as I'm sure a farmer would have been very proud of a son or daughter who could toil in the soil all day long.)

I feel society can be too quick to offer a magic solution through a pill, just because a child can't sit still in class. I realise this is simplistic — but, well, who would want to? A whole world is out there to explore!

I know exactly why movement is so important for me — physically, yes, but mentally so much more. As a kid, like many of us growing up, I was always out until the streetlights came on. Even as a teenager, I remember waking up at the crack of dawn to wax my surfboard and paddle out through the waves, sitting beyond the break as the sun rose, floating in the ocean and having a good chat to the other surfers.

Feeling the benefits of movement

Moving your body is essential for physical wellbeing, helping to prevent chronic illnesses such as diabetes and cardiovascular disease. But it's also extremely beneficial for your mind, increasing productivity and creativity, while boosting your mood and improving your mental health. Movement gets those happy chemicals firing in your brain, helping you to feel happier, more relaxed and less stressed. And, as the cherry on top, regular aerobic movement (which gets your heart pumping) has also been shown to protect memory and improve thinking skills and learning[32] and slow cognitive decline.[33]

Movement improves your wellbeing by:

- making you less stressed
- giving you more energy
- boosting personal confidence and self-awareness
- improving concentration and learning
- reducing feelings of depression and anxiety
- making you happier
- improving bone health and cognitive function
- improving your quality of sleep.

But let's drill down a little on those 'happy chemicals'. When you move your body, the neurotransmitters endorphins, dopamine and serotonin are released. These naturally occurring chemicals are important to many functions in the brain, body and emotions. Neurotransmitters play a key role in the function of the central nervous system by passing signals from one neuron to the next.

Think about neurotransmitters as being the highway from the brain to the body—and the right combination of chemicals travelling along the highway, at the right speed, to the right destination, the better overall performance the body will have.

Scientific evidence confirms that physical activity improves brain health and cognitive function at any age. Studies are now also showing levels of the protein known as brain-derived neurotrophic factor (BDNF) is increased through exercise and movement. BDNF helps make the brain cells stronger, healthier, better connected and larger, which leads to increased learning capabilities, and can act against anxiety and depression.[34]

So whenever you are feeling negative, instead of dwelling in it, try to get up and get moving—outside, if possible. Taking a break to go outside, get some fresh air and move can really improve your mood.

Another important takeaway here is to do something that's fun and that you enjoy, so it's sustainable. I once signed up for a boot camp, and got myself out of bed and down to the foreshore for a 6 am session. For the next 60 minutes, I was yelled at to do this and do that and sweat more and hurry up. Perhaps this sounds like a perfect start to the day for you, but I felt like I was being punished!

I realised I had to *enjoy* movement for it to be a staple in my life. Movement for you can include exercise, sport or a hobby, but make sure you can do it daily where possible—and you'll be far more consistent when it includes others and fun. Instead of making your exercise sessions serious, try to make them enjoyable. Add some music, for example, take a challenge with friends or have a social catch-up afterwards (perhaps so you can complain about how hard it was).

TAKING ACTION

By making movement a natural part of the workday, you can boost energy, mood and overall performance, while reducing stress and fatigue. So get yourself—and your team—moving!

MOVEMENT ACTIVITIES

Start of the day:

- Morning movement activation with light stretches or breathwork before starting work.
- Walk or bike to work, if possible.
- Take the stairs instead of the elevator.

During work hours:

- Use active workstations such as standing desks, stability balls or balance boards.
- Walk and talk during phone calls or meetings.
- Set a timer every 50 minutes for a quick stand, stretch or short walk.
- Do desk exercises such as calf raises, squats, seated leg lifts or shoulder rolls.
- Walk and talk to a colleague in the same office instead of emailing them.

Meetings and collaboration:

- Conduct walking meetings outdoors or around the office.
- Keep short team meetings standing to promote energy and focus.

- Organise quick stretching or breathing exercises before or after meetings.

Afternoon energy boost:

- Take a post-lunch walk outside to get some fresh air.

- Do chair yoga or mobility work at your desk.

- Stand up and shake it out before switching tasks to reset focus.

- Plan light exercise, stretching or yoga after work.

TIME FOR ACTION QUESTIONS

- What do you love to do that involves movement?

- What kind of movement can you do with others?

- What can you do to include movement in your daily rhythm?

LET'S MAKE IT HAPPEN!

Take one minute to set an intention to do one thing today to move. Put it in your diary, phone a friend and lock it in!

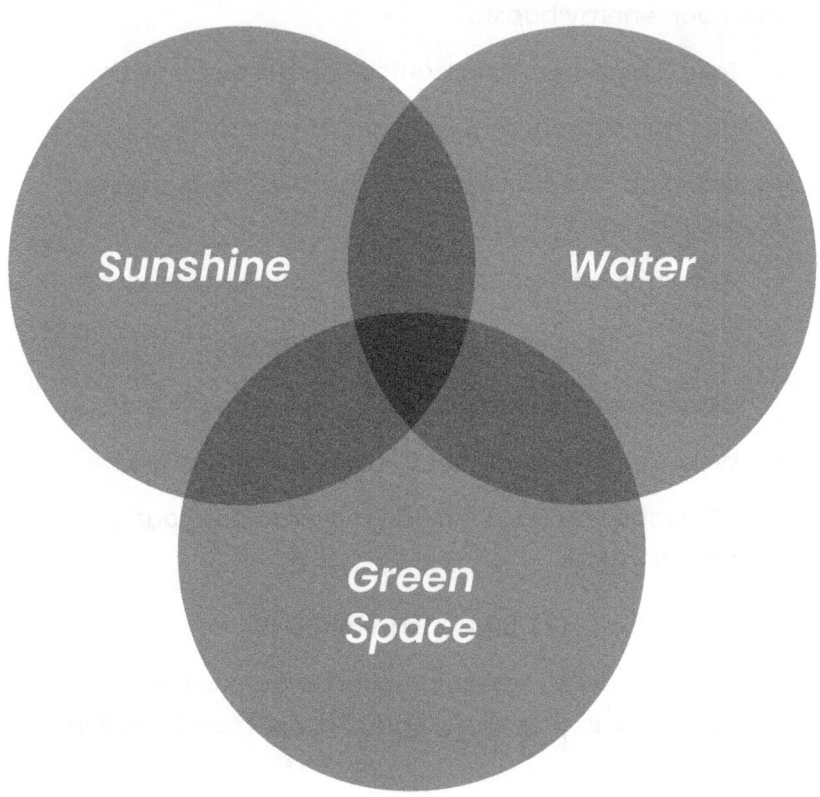

Elements of the environment GreenX7 tool

Chapter 13
Environment

For as long as I can remember, I've enjoyed nature — whether it's been for fun, adventure, work, reflection or healing. Innately, I just knew that nature was where I needed to be. You could even say I'm an addict, because I'm constantly looking for a nature fix every day!

Even today is a case in point — it's 11.32 am and I should have been at my desk at 9.00 am, writing this book. Instead, I went for a surf. I just can't help myself. I'm constantly thinking about how I can coordinate my work around playing outside — and even when I'm working, I'm still trying to find ways to run my workshops, keynotes or consultation sessions outdoors. Luckily, my wife, Carly, is the same; otherwise, we would never see each other. But I no longer feel guilty about 'giving in' to this need, because I know nature is where I find my inspiration, creativity, joy and the fuel I need to recharge my battery so I can continually thrive sustainably. With the help of science, experts are now proving what we all feel — that being in nature not only feels good but can also heal us mentally, emotionally, physically and spiritually. It's a medicine cabinet for so many of our ailments.

Finding time for nature

Spending time in nature — whether in green spaces, near water, or among towering evergreen trees — has a profound impact on our emotional, physical, and mental wellbeing. No doubt you instinctively know that being in nature helps you feel more relaxed, but scientists now have the data to explain why.

Evergreen trees, pine trees and other plants release natural compounds called phytoncides, which have been shown to reduce stress by lowering cortisol levels and improve immune function. Studies also link time spent in forest environments to lower blood pressure, supporting better heart health. Similarly, exposure to natural settings such as parks, forests, and bodies of water has been found to improve mood, reduce anxiety and enhance overall wellbeing.[35]

More specifically, having contact with your natural environment improves your wellbeing by:

- reducing stress (lowering cortisol)
- reducing your blood pressure, heart rate and muscle tension
- reducing anxiety and depression
- increasing your personal energy
- increasing your vitamin D production
- improving your memory performance and attention span
- improving your self-esteem.

Being in nature just makes you feel good!

While these benefits are well-documented, they typically build over time rather than happening instantly. This means the more you immerse yourself in nature, the more you experience its restorative effects — making it a simple yet powerful way to support long-term health and happiness.

Your natural environment can be accessed almost anywhere, anytime, and for free. The types of natural environments and conditions that can recharge your batteries are:

- *Green spaces:* Natural places with lots of green foliage, such as parks, forests and gardens.

- *Sunshine:* Exposure to direct sunlight each day.

- *Water:* Natural water sources, such as oceans, rivers, fountains and ponds.

If you can combine all three aspects — for example, by being at the beach — you can enhance the benefits.

You can even combine your daily movement with your favourite green space to, again, enhance the effects — instead of just walking on a treadmill bounded by the monotony of four walls, for example.

This combination of movement and green spaces is now known as 'green exercise'. Coined in 2005 by Professor Jules Pretty, green exercise refers to any physical exercise undertaken in natural environments. Studies by Professor Pretty and his co-researchers have also highlighted the potentially synergistic wellbeing benefits arising from activity in green or natural places.[36]

Other researchers have also highlighted the benefits of green exercise. According to a 2011 study from Jo Thompson

Coon and others at the University of Exeter, 'exercising in natural environments was associated with greater feelings of revitalization and positive engagement, decreases in tension, confusion, anger, and depression, and increased energy'.[37]

Let's now take a look at the three types of environmental spaces and conditions — green spaces sunshine and water — in a little more detail.

Green spaces

A green space is a natural outdoor environment, such as a park, botanical garden, playground, an oval, bushland or even your backyard. It is any space with a lot of naturally occurring green foliage. These green spaces are amazing resources that not only improve our mood and self-esteem but also restore our ability to concentrate. Improved concentration of course, is essential for quality planning, problem solving, goal setting and engaging in effective social interactions.

So have a think about ways you can step outside your home or office more often and embrace the great outdoors. Think about the spaces you could use each day and the environments you move through. Which environments steal your energy (deplete you) and which environments give you energy (recharge you)? You can probably think of environments — and people — that do both. However, what you likely innately know is that the natural environment is one of the best ways to recharge your battery.

And while we are on the subject of the natural world, a quick advertisement break brought to you on behalf of planet Earth!

When considering your connection with your natural environment and outdoor spaces, also consider the example you are setting for future generations (either directly or more generally). As our children spend more time indoors and less time connecting with the outdoors, they can start to see our natural environment as a 'nice to have' rather than a need. This same generation that will one day be 'commander and chief' — and, with no connection to the environment, may not think twice about destroying our natural playgrounds to further capitalism. We need to help foster and restore our connection with our natural environment, and bring our children along on the journey, to encourage greater stewardship of the environment. This will improve not only our wellbeing but also the wellbeing of our planet.

Sunshine

Humans spend less time in the sun today than at any other point throughout our history, and this is having an adverse effect on our health. While this is in part due to people's (valid) concerns about the rising rates of skin cancer, our indoor lifestyles are also to blame. Many of us work in office jobs that keep us inside for most of the day, and then we return home to watch screens for our down time.

While a cautious approach with sun exposure during the peak UV periods is warranted, I really think we have tilted the scales too much towards being indoor, sedentary creatures. Exposure to direct sunlight (and especially the UVB ultraviolet rays) can be very good for us for short periods of time. UVB rays help our bodies make vitamin D, needed for many physical and psychological processes.

For individuals with fair skin, exposing the arms and legs to sunlight for approximately 10 to 15 minutes daily is generally sufficient to produce the recommended amount of vitamin D.

Those with darker skin tones may require longer exposure due to higher melanin levels, which can reduce the skin's ability to synthesise vitamin D. The optimal time for vitamin D production is around midday, typically between 10.00 am and 2.00 pm, when UVB rays are most intense. However, these are also the times when exposure to the sun can cause the most damage, so it's important to balance sun exposure with skin cancer risk by using appropriate sun protection measures after sufficient exposure. Also keep in mind that, even in the late afternoon, some vitamin D production can occur, especially during summer months.

Sunshine generally can improve your overall wellbeing by:

- improving your mood
- improving your immune function
- triggering alertness and vitality
- regulating the inflammatory response
- supporting the prevention of many chronic diseases and illnesses.[38]

Perhaps you're old enough to remember a certain advertising campaign advising all Australians not go out into the sunshine — and if you did, you always had to 'slip, slop, slap'. (I even remember the song that went with it, so catchy!) I wonder if they could create another campaign to get Aussies back outdoors ...

Water

Being in, around or just looking at moving water can supply a great dose of natural medicine. Negative ions are found in abundance in nature especially near a waterfall, river or at the beach. Negative ions counterbalance the positive ions emitted by cars, computers, televisions, mobile devices and other aspects of our technology rich lives. Negative ions increase the flow of oxygen in the brain, resulting in higher alertness, decreased drowsiness and more mental energy.[39]

Waterfalls have the highest production of negative ions (between 95000 and 450000 ions measurable) while air conditioners have a very low production of negative ions (0 to 20 ions measurable). Think about how you feel while stuck in an air-conditioned office with no circulating fresh air and limited views of nature, compared to being in a park or at the beach.

The negative ions in natural water sources can improve our wellbeing by:

- decreasing our feelings of stress and anxiety
- increasing our energy and mood
- improving our task performance.

TAKING ACTION

Time to get outside and re-establish your connection with your natural environment — even while at work.

NATURE CONNECTION ACTIVITIES

At work:

- Hold walking meetings outdoors or in green spaces.
- Set up a workplace garden or indoor plants to enhance those innate positive responses people have for living things.

(continued)

- Encourage lunch breaks outside in a natural setting.
- Introduce 'reconnect hours' for employees to spend time in nature.
- Organise outdoor team-building activities such as hikes or park workouts.
- Allow flexible workstations with access to outdoor seating areas.
- Schedule nature-based mindfulness or meditation sessions.
- Open windows for natural light and fresh air circulation.
- Use nature sounds or visual elements (such as posters or desktop backgrounds) to bring nature indoors.

At home:

- Take morning or evening walks in a park or near water.
- Create a small home garden or indoor plant corner.
- Do yoga, stretching or workouts outside.
- Plan weekly outdoor activities such as hiking, biking or beach visits.
- Eat meals outside on a balcony, patio or in a park.
- Schedule tech-free nature breaks, such as 15 minutes of mindful outdoor time.
- Read, journal or meditate in a natural setting.
- Listen to nature sounds instead of artificial background noise.

- Use natural materials in home decor (including wood, stone and plants) to enhance connection with nature.

TIME FOR ACTION QUESTIONS

- How much sunlight do you get each day? Do you need more?

- What green spaces and/or water do you have access to, near work or home?

- What could you do to include some outdoor time into your daily rhythm?

LET'S MAKE IT HAPPEN!

Take one minute to set an intention to get some outdoor time today and this week. Put it in your diary, phone a friend and lock it in! Recharge your battery!

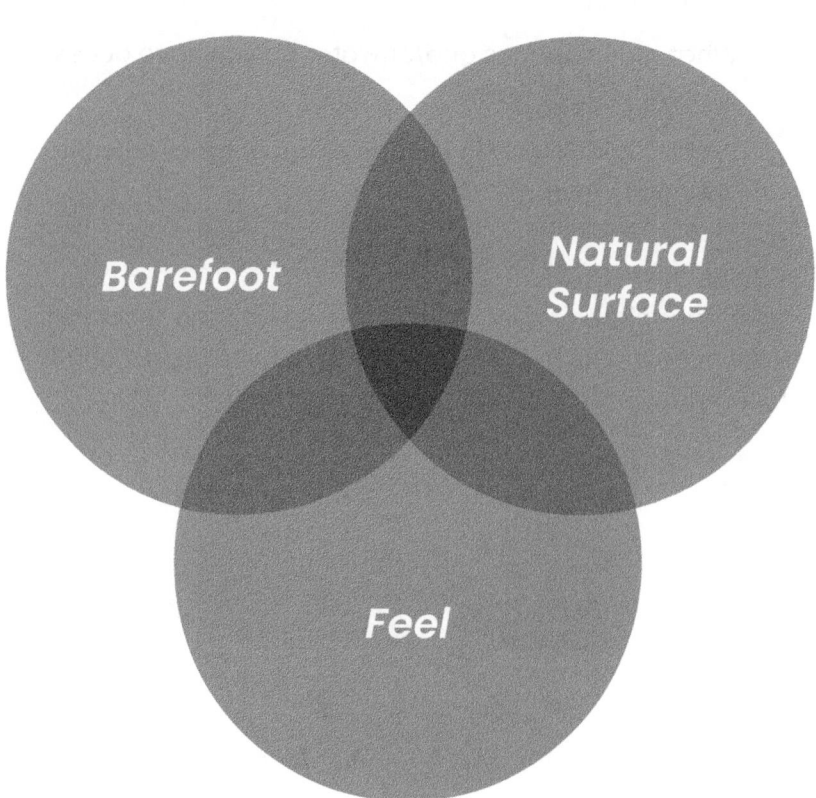

Elements of the earthing GreenX7 tool

Chapter 14
Earthing

When I first started researching the science behind what would become the GreenX7 tools, I knew I was the perfect guinea pig when it came to studying the benefits of active engagement in nature. At the age of 21, freshly returned from my overseas backpacking adventures, I walked into an old airport hangar with a sign above that read Kirra Dive. I had dreadlocks, the best tan of my life and had decided I wanted to be a divemaster! From that moment on, and still to this day, shoes are my last option. I have always preferred to be barefoot.

Even now when I run workshops or keynotes, I'm always looking for an angle to get the audience to take off their shoes so I can do the same. So back in 2013 when I was researching the tools for everyday wellness, I instinctively started to look at my own habits and wondered if they had any scientific evidence to back up how I felt when following them. Looking down at my (bare) feet seemed a good foundational place to start with my research — and what I found blew me away.

The universal power of earthing

Another reason for finding research to back up what I already innately knew was my corporate work. I knew that if I was going to go into this landscape and tell people to take off their shoes, I better have a good reason for them to do so.

I'll never forget a meeting I had with the head of the Australian Army Soldier Recovery Centre. I was there to discuss the course content that I would be facilitating to their soldiers — and out of all of the GreenX7 tools we had created, earthing was the one that I thought could be really seen as 'fluffy tree hugging' hippy stuff. So even though I had the research to back up the benefit, I was still sweating bullets (mind the pun) when I came around to discussing it with the course director. In my deepest, most authoritarian voice, I began by saying, 'Let me discuss our third tool called earthing ... '

Straightaway, he stopped me. *Uh-oh*, I thought, *this isn't good*. But he just said, 'Tim, skip to the next tool please. We've just watched a documentary on earthing, and I can see the benefits. So I'm happy to have this included in your workshop'. Phew!

What was crazier was then getting a bunch of soldiers to unstrap their boots and frolic barefoot on the grass. Luckily I grew up in a family of boys and could easily diffuse the situation with humour, but earthing remained a tough sell in some workshops — until the coach of the NSW Blues NRL team started adding this into his practice sessions, getting his team to walk barefoot on the footy field.

I had to realise that something that was so common to me could be so alien to someone else, and could really push them out of their comfort zone. As an example of this, I was hosting a leadership retreat off an island of Hong Kong for Cordis Hotel. I got the team outside and asked them to take off their shoes. While they were doing so, I asked them how long it had been since they felt their bare feet on a natural surface. For so many of them, it had been many years; however, one lady said it had been over 30 years! I almost fell over. How could someone be so disconnected from the Earth for so long? Perhaps if you've ever been to Hong Kong, it makes sense to you, but I still couldn't understand it.

What was more magical than seeing the team's faces as they walked barefoot, connected to nature, was Cordis going on to create an earthing area for their staff and guests outside their entrance in the heart of Mong Kok, one of the major shopping areas in Hong Kong. With land prices in Hong Kong being the most expensive on the planet, that five-by-three-metre space is probably worth more than my local shopping mall! The beauty about earthing, and why it has such a significant impact on people, is that it has the ability to get us out of our heads and allow us the opportunity to feel our body and be present.

Our bodies have a type of electrical current pulsing through them, and connecting with the Earth's negative charges can create a stable internal bioelectrical environment for the functioning of all our body systems. Your brain, heartbeat and neurotransmitter activity all rely on electrical signals. If your own current is 'off', certain aspects of your health can be as well. Having direct contact with the Earth's surface can help reset your biological balance. The Earth's surface holds its own energy source, with the free-flowing electrons constantly replenished by solar radiation and lightning. Connecting with this energy promotes health, harmonises and stabilises the body's basic biological rhythms, and can neutralise inflammation.

Earthing allows the free-flowing electrons from the Earth's surface to be absorbed through the soles of our feet, and provides the following benefits:

- reducing stress and anxiety
- reducing inflammation
- reducing pain
- speeding up wound healing
- improving our sleep
- increasing our energy.[40]

As the authors of *Earthing: The Most Important Health Discovery Ever?* noted,

> Physical disconnect with the earth creates abnormal physiology and contributes to inflammation, pain, fatigue, stress and poor sleep. By reconnecting to the earth's natural surface, symptoms are rapidly relieved and even eliminated, and recovery from surgery, injury and athlete overexertion is accelerated.[41]

Earthing is simply taking your shoes off and putting your bare feet on the ground. This may sound simple, but when was the last time you did it? For me, I enjoy the break I get from disconnecting from all the thoughts running through my mind, and allowing my body to feel again through focusing on the different textures underneath my feet — whether this is from sand, grass, rocks or dirt. It's also a great way to whittle away time with the kids.

TAKING ACTION

When was the last time you were barefoot in nature? What does it remind you of and how does it make you feel? Can you get back there today? Can you help your team do the same?

EARTHING ACTIVITIES

At work:

- Create outdoor break areas with grass or natural surfaces for barefoot grounding.

- Encourage your team to take short barefoot walks during breaks.

- Organise outdoor meetings in grassy or sandy areas.

- Provide indoor grounding mats for those who can't go outside. (Grounding mats provide a conductive surface designed to connect your body to the Earth, mimicking the benefits of walking barefoot outside.)

- Incorporate earthing into wellness programs, including lunchtime grounding sessions.

- Encourage stretching or meditation sessions outdoors on natural surfaces.

- Use natural flooring materials such as wooden floors or stone pathways where possible.

- Promote 'earthing challenges', where employees track time spent grounding.

- Allow flexible workspace options with outdoor seating near grass or soil.

(continued)

- Introduce nature-based mindfulness breaks, emphasising barefoot grounding.

At home:

- Walk barefoot in the garden, grass, sand or soil for a few minutes daily.

- Start mornings with a short outdoor barefoot walk.

- Spend time gardening without shoes to connect with the earth.

- Do yoga, stretching or meditation on natural surfaces outdoors.

- Sit or lie on the ground while reading, relaxing or spending time outside.

- Use earthing mats indoors for grounding benefits while working or sleeping.

- Encourage kids and family members to play barefoot outdoors.

- Take vacations or weekend trips to nature spots with accessible grounding surfaces.

- Walk on the beach or in shallow water for a natural grounding experience.

- Reduce synthetic footwear use at home to increase barefoot time.

TIME FOR ACTION QUESTIONS

- Where can you access a natural place to go barefoot?

- What can you do to include it in your daily rhythm?

LET'S MAKE IT HAPPEN!

Take one minute to set an intention to do some earthing today or this week. Put it in your diary, phone a friend and lock it in! Recharge your battery!

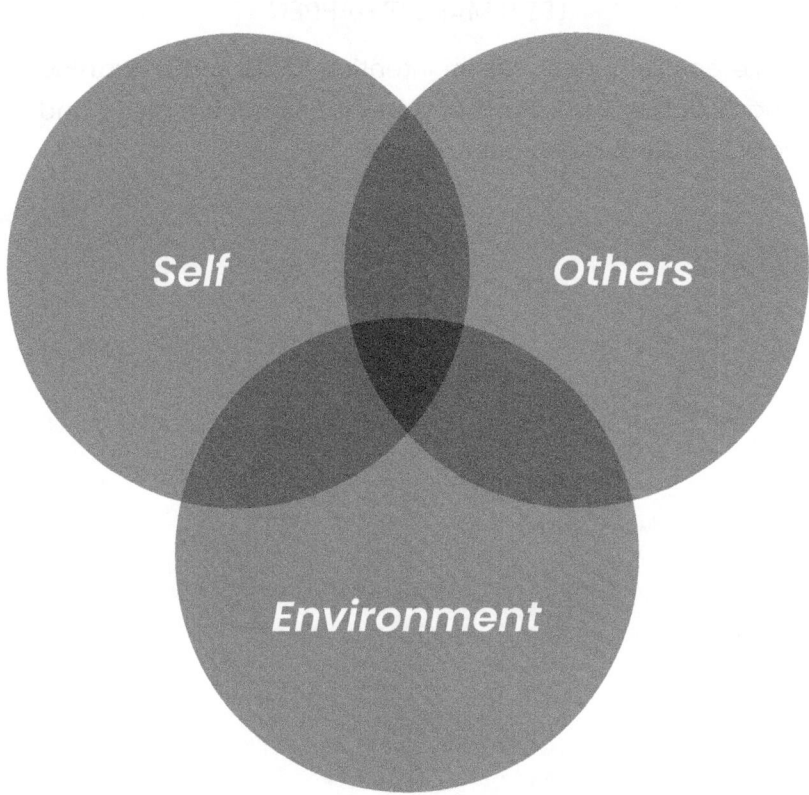

Elements in the time GreenX7 tool

Chapter 15

Time

I'm often asked for that first step I'd recommend for someone to start to thrive sustainably. My answer always comes back to something along the lines of, 'You need to make time'. Funnily enough, this always seems to be the answer that no-one wants to hear. As a society, many of us in the Western world seem to take the prescription before the prevention route. We work ourselves to the bone until we end up sick and tired and can't get out of bed, turning to medication to help. Too many of us have surrendered to the idea of simply surviving or functioning, instead of wanting to thrive. I want to turn this around. I don't want you going through your life day by day in a mediocre fashion, thinking that by the end of each week, each year and at the end of your life you're going to somehow be content with what could be your one and only chance to leave your mark on this planet.

So, yes, you need to make time!

How do you do that, you ask? A great question.

Giving yourself the freedom of time

When the global financial crisis (GFC) hit in 2008, I was still a divemaster, taking wealthy clients on wonderful adventures at home and abroad. I was always envious of their lifestyles and their ability to just come away and play. It wasn't until the GFC hit that I realised that most of this 'wealth' was all smoke and mirrors. Behind the scenes, many of these clients were like the proverbial duck on the water — serene and calm above, and scrambling like crazy underneath. Many people lost not only their fortunes during the GFC, but also their families, and many lost their health from the side effects. What I didn't know then (but do know now) is too many of these people had not prioritised their time to look after themselves, their family or their health. Instead, they had focused their time on the accumulation of things rather than memories.

One of my mentors at the time was Gaz, or who I affectionately referred to as 'Dive Dad'. He managed to glide through the crises after a few bumps and continued. I admired Gaz because he seemed to always be grounded and have it together both professionally and personally. I remember asking him for advice as to how he managed to pull through when everyone else seemed to flail or fail. As I mention in chapter 1, the advice he gave me became a core foundation for how I live my life today.

'Timbo, you always need to live well within your means.'

What he meant was to purchase things you can easily afford. Whether you're buying a house, car, holiday or anything else, you need to make sure that you're always living well within your means, because this allows you financial freedom — which then allows you time.

If you're constantly scraping through week by week, you're either having to work above and beyond, which is unhealthy, or your brain is working too hard, worrying about how to pay it all off. I'm not suggesting you don't strive for the good life — although we could debate about what the 'good life' really entails — but I'm asking you to consider how you can slow down and allow yourself time. Remember that phrase 'be the turtle' I mention in chapter 1, and the turtle's sense of calm and 'go with the flow' attitude. This way, when you do reach your financial goals, you will still have your health and family there to enjoy it with you.

How do you spend your time? The following figure shows a weekly breakdown for an average Australian, based on data from the Australian Bureau of Statistics. For this example, I've chosen someone in a similar demographic to me who would have similar commitments with a family and work responsibilities — a white-collar city employee with a family.

As shown in the figure, the weekly time allocation breaks down as follows:

- *Sleep:* 56 hours.
- *Work:* 40 hours.
- *Chores:* 14 hours.

- *Commute:* 6 hours.

- *Cooking and eating:* 14 hours.

- *Grooming:* 3 hours.

- *Entertainment:* 7 hours.

- *Social media and screen time:* 25 hours.

- *Time for self and others:* 3 hours.[42]

The first thing that surprised me from this weekly breakdown was just how much time we spend on chores. I had guessed it would be around an hour a day, but the numbers show it's more like 14 hours per week — almost two full workdays dedicated to keeping life in order.

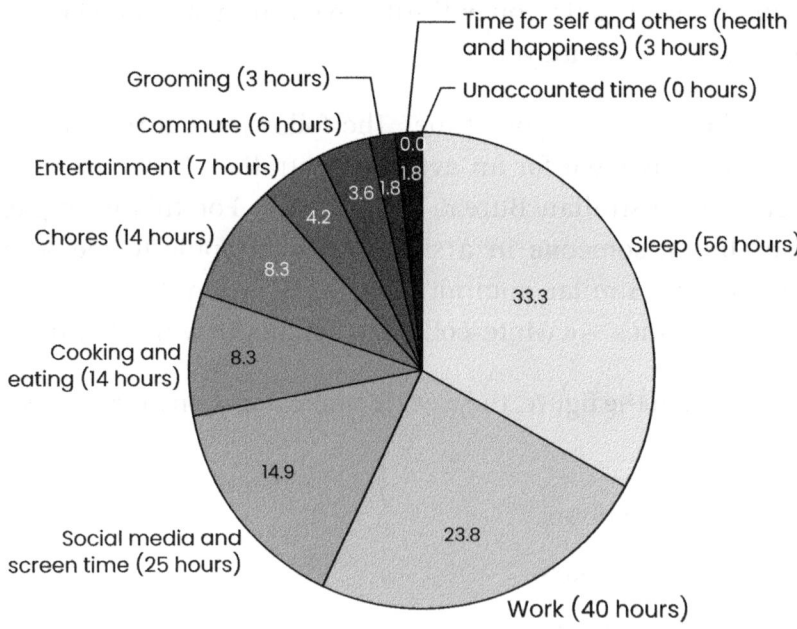

Weekly time allocation for an average Australian parent

What really stands out, though, is how little time we spend on what truly matters. We dedicate 32 hours a week to screens and entertainment — watching, scrolling, and spectating — yet only three hours to connecting with ourselves and our loved ones.

Then there's work. At around 40 hours a week, you still have some space for balance, but what happens when that stretches to 50 or 60 hours? Maybe you're already there. And, if so, what have you noticed slipping away? Usually, it's time for yourself first, then time with family and friends, then proper meals and, eventually, sleep. The more you push past 60-hour work weeks, the more life starts to feel like it's running on autopilot, leaving little energy for anything else.

For some, working long hours is unavoidable — perhaps you're a C-suite executive, an entrepreneur, or simply escaping the chaos of home for the quiet of the office. But at what cost? And if this is your reality, how do you protect the time you do have so that you're not just surviving, but actually living?

I'd like you to reflect on where your time is being spent. Are you making the best of that time in the short, medium and long term? Sometimes it's easier to plonk yourself on a couch, veg out and scroll away your time. But what if you stole back some of those 32 hours (and possibly up to 46 hours[43]) a week spectating on a screen and put them to increase those three hours a week to prioritise yourself and others.

Ask yourself:

- How do you prioritise your time?
- Do you make time each day to take care of your own wellbeing?

- Are you spending your time on the things that really matter in the short, medium and long term?

When COVID hit, we had to press pause on almost all our GreenX7 contracts due to the face-to-face nature of our workshops and events, and working internationally with many of our clients. We were lucky that we had our app and online challenge to help us scrape through, but that same year my first child, Sonny, was born. This was when the philosophy of 'living within your means' truly paid dividends — even though we still had to run our companies, and with that came overheads, we were still in a financial position that allowed me to have six months downtime to be the best husband and father I could be to Carly and Sonny. I allowed myself to take the foot off the accelerator and enjoy those months of precious moments that I will cherish forever.

We can always make more money, but we can never make more time.

Taking time to 'be' rather than 'do'

Many of the people I coach tell me they don't have the time to take better care of their own wellbeing. They can't afford to get anymore sleep, spend 30 minutes exercising or just stop for 30 minutes a day to sit down with themselves, partner or family to reconnect and reflect. When I ask them why they work themselves so hard, they usually explain it's because they want their family and themselves to be happy.

We are always so busy 'doing'. When we factor in time for work, travel, sleep, parenting commitments and daily tasks, we can see how our day rapidly fills up. How can you take your foot off the accelerator and just 'be' rather than 'do'?

Could it be that you are looking at time in the wrong way? Maybe it's not that you don't have enough time but that you are not prioritizing yourself in your own life. We all have the same amount of time; it's about making the deliberate effort to make the time to look after you.

What happens if your battery is constantly in function/survival mode and you get sick or burnout? Who is going to look after everything then? When we get on a plane, we are always told to put on our oxygen mask in the case of an emergency before helping anyone else. We should literally be doing this in our own lives.

Before starting GreenX7, I wasn't who I am now, and I wasn't thriving sustainably or growing into the best version of myself. I finally realised that before I could help anyone else, before I could give them the best of what I had, I had to recharge my own battery first. So, these days, I make sure that I connect to the GreenX7 tools to be able to do that.

Think about those moments throughout the day when you can take some time for you, take your foot off the accelerator, stop doing and just be. Take time to reconnect to yourself, friends and family, and to reconnect to the amazing natural environment around you. What time during the day is good for you to reconnect to recharge — morning, lunch, afternoon or evening? Be specific, or it probably won't happen. You need to build a routine to create time for yourself each day to look after you.

My time for looking after me and just being is 6.45 to 8.30 am. I am strict about keeping that time for myself and my family, and use it to get outside, go to the beach or park, and allow myself to breathe.

You have the ability to make informed choices, and to develop habits that are good for your overall health. Your choice to make time for self, others and nature for your everyday wellness does need to be deliberate. If you prioritise time for yourself, however, you give yourself the opportunity to become the best you can be. Again, when you look after yourself, you are better able to support the people in your life.

Once again, this is all about connecting to self, others and nature. So take the time:

- *Time for self:* Time to 'just be' and not be always doing, to recharge your batteries first so you have more vitality to help others and thrive sustainably. The most important person in your life is you. When you take the time to nurture and support yourself, you can care, support and inspire others.

- *Time for others:* Allow time to be present in the company of others, to make them feel valued. Research shows that the warmth of relationships is what gives us life's greatest satisfaction — and can have a powerful influence on our health.[44]

- *Time for nature:* Making time to be in nature not only feels good but also has significant benefits to your physical, mental and emotional wellbeing (as highlighted in the previous two chapters), and allows you to understand what's important for you.

You can use your time more intentionally by:

- being aware of what your body needs
- providing a balance of activity and inactivity
- taking the opportunity to live in the now and just be
- increasing your awareness of life goals.

TAKING ACTION

Give yourself the freedom of time, to just 'be' and to recharge. Find ways through your workday that you and your team can do the same.

TIME RELATED ACTIVITIES

At work:

- Use five-minute focus resets through the day, by setting a timer for five minutes to breathe, stretch, or walk outside before switching tasks.

- Dedicate one 'power hour' to deep, distraction-free work before checking emails or social media.

- Track your (and your team's) energy levels throughout the day and align demanding tasks with peak focus times.

- Encourage two-minute 'micro break' resets such as desk stretches, eye relaxation or a quick walk.

- Take a 30-second pause between meetings to reset mentally and intentionally transition before the next task.

(continued)

- Implement 'no meeting mornings' by blocking off a morning each week for uninterrupted, high-focus work for yourself and your team.

- Before moving to a new task, take three deep breaths to stay present and mindfully switch.

At home:

- Dedicate time to step outside and observe natural light shifts, and the sunrise and sunset.

- Spend the first few minutes of a meal in silence, mindfully focusing on taste and gratitude.

- Set specific hours of tech-free time when no screens are allowed, to encourage presence.

- Dedicate one hour per week to being a 'slow hour' — moving slowly and mindfully, without rushing.

- Journal for five minutes each day, reflecting on one highlight and one lesson from the day.

- Set a reminder 'wind-down alarm' an hour before bed to shift into relaxation mode.

- Take a three-second pause before answering calls, texts or emails to stay mindful.

TIME FOR ACTION QUESTIONS

- What is stopping you from doing the things you love and taking good care of yourself?

- Do you make yourself a priority in your own life?

- How do you spend your down time?

- What time of day could you use to reconnect to recharge?

- Make a time log and see how you spend your day.

LET'S MAKE IT HAPPEN!

Create a plan for how you will prioritise your wellbeing today — and do it!

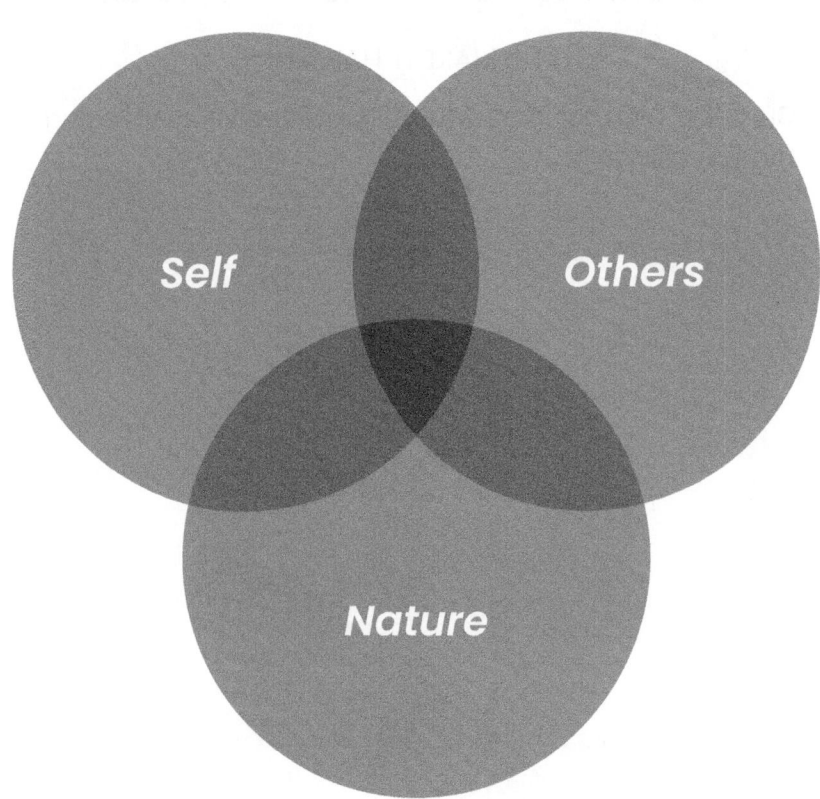

Elements in the connection GreenX7 tool

Chapter 16
Connection

Over the years, I've learned the hard way about the difference between *communication* and *connection*, and I've lost some great people along the journey because of it. The word 'connection' wasn't really in my vocabulary. I'm not sure if every time I heard it, I wrote it off as 'fluffy' or I was just never taught its importance. Whatever the reason, like most important lessons in my life, I learned about connection through the school of hard knocks.

One of the reasons I'm writing this book is so I can pass down lessons like this to my kids and give them a head start in life (hopefully with fewer of the 'hard knocks'). What I know now is that, for me, *communication* is the ability to get your message across, while *connection* is the ability for your message to be heard, felt and connected to. Communication is skin deep, whereas connection resonates with the heart.

Connecting through being present

One of my greatest weaknesses in life has now become one of my greatest strengths, and that is the ability to connect. To connect, you also need the ability to actively listen, and this is complemented through your body language. You need to be totally present. You need to sustain eye contact, and to feel like your body is reaching out to that person like a virtual hug to create a feeling of being valued for the other person.

I see you, and I hear you.

At the end of the day, we all just want to feel valued, have a sense of meaning and feel like we belong. Creating a connection with someone helps create these feelings, which helps create self-worth and, in turn, self-love. This is what we all need to want to look after ourselves and thrive sustainably.

One of the biggest shifts in my relationships that has come through connection is simply the way I greet my wife, Carly, when she gets home, and vice versa. In the past, when my partner walked through the door, the old me would have continued to watch TV, play on my phone or tap away at the keyboard. I may have asked, 'How was your day?' But I wouldn't have really cared about the response — not an amazing way to make the person you love feel loved.

The new me — the Tim who values connection because he's finally worked out how important it is — greets Carly as follows. When I hear Carly enter the gate at home, I stop whatever I'm doing and open the door to greet her with a big smile, hug and kiss. Yesterday, she had been catching up with one of her friends who had just had a baby boy, Wilby. So I asked her, 'How did you go at Lucy's, and how is Wilby?' Then I just listened for a few minutes. This seemingly simple interaction is an extremely powerful act, because it creates value, meaning and belonging for your partner. What it also creates is a 'cause and effect' scenario, where Carly, as she walks through the gate, gets a warm, loving feeling, knowing what's about to greet her.

We also make sure we connect over dinner, by switching off all our devices, throwing some dinner tunes on, lighting a candle and trying to create some resemblance of a romantic dinner. Now I get that if you have kids, this could be an almost impossible task — but it's worth a try, right?

What we are focused on is creating interactions throughout our day that make us and those around us feel valued — whether that's our family and friends, neighbours, colleagues or even the barista. It's a win–win scenario for both parties, and helps recharge our batteries.

Positive human connection creates value, meaning and belonging in our lives. This gives us self-worth, which gives us the love we need to want to look after ourselves — and the research backs this up.

The Harvard Study of Adult Development (previously known as the Grant Study) has been tracking the health of 268 Harvard male sophomores since 1938, hoping to discover clues to leading healthy and happy lives. The study, which continues to track the surviving men and now the offspring of the original cohort, revealed a surprising finding: 'Close relationships, more than money or fame, are what keep people happy throughout their lives'.[45] This finding caused George Vaillant, who directed the study for more than three decades, to conclude that the warmth of relationships is what gives us life's greatest satisfaction — and that, 'it was a history of warm intimate relationships — and the ability to foster them in maturity — that predicted flourishing in all aspects of these men's lives'.[46]

From all the research I have done around wellbeing over the years Vaillant's conclusions were the most profound I had read. They fundamentally changed the lens through which I looked at wellness. I moved from not just creating action-based habits to looking at feeling-based habits. The findings of this study changed my purpose, values and daily focus, as I realised that I could do something that would improve not only my own wellbeing but also the wellbeing of others.

Disconnecting to reconnect

Research shows that we are more reliant on social media to try to create our self-worth, and less reliant on the people around us to help us. In 2016, a national survey conducted by suicide-prevention organisation R U OK? found that respondents spent an average of 46 hours a week looking at screens, compared to just six hours connecting with family and friends.[47] Many of us are now more inclined to stay indoors on our devices, and less inclined to go outdoors and enjoy the environment we live in. By doing so, we're missing out on our chance to connect with neighbours, those within your community, sometimes even our friends and family.

I completely understand that if you're in a foul mood or feeling emotional, you're unlikely to venture out and reveal yourself to the world. Wanting to connect with people can be difficult, and you no doubt prefer to keep your scowl or teary face hidden away. Life gets tough sometimes, and sometimes it's tough all the time. You can think and feel like you just can't catch a break, the world is against you and your 'unflappable' resilience is starting to feel completely flappable. You can get tired, exhausted and just feel like throwing in the towel. No matter how many cups of tea you have, the saying 'everything feels better after a cuppa' starts to sound like nonsense.

When you feel like this, I get it. All you want to do when you come home is zone out in front of one of the many devices that allow you to escape from your less than perfect world and let you live a fantasy life through someone else. With your popcorn and chocolate and a remote in your hand, this can feel like a great respite, one that wields unfathomable power to indulge you in spectatorship. I'm not knocking this need — in fact, every once in a while I'm sitting right there with you, indulging in my escapism.

Problems arise, however, when you look forward to living life through the lens of someone else instead of living your own, and when you would prefer to watch someone else's 'hero's journey' rather than create our own. The problems deepen when you turn your back on those you love and love you, when you're both tired and exhausted and you say some words you now regret. You wait for the other person to apologise and what started as a crack soon becomes a chasm. You know that the only thing that will pull you back together is a long, embracing hug and the words 'I'm sorry' — but these actions get harder and harder.

When you feel like you're at your lowest point, the last thing you may wish to do is connect with another human being. However, the thing you need most is that warmth of relationship that fills your heart with love, security, value, meaning, belonging and so many other things that you need to pull yourself up and out of the cave that you have been hiding in. And that warmth isn't found through likes on a screen or someone sending you a fire emoji because you posted a photo of you looking devilishly handsome. That deep inner hug of the heart comes from having someone look fully at you, and you feeling that they care, and that they see you and hear you. This is what can bring you back from that dark, unfathomable cave that you have perhaps ended up in, lost without a compass and map. Other human beings are your guiding light out.

Although we are more connected to each other through technology than any previous generation, we have also become more isolated. Our lack of real connection to others is leading to loneliness, depression and even suicide. We are not getting the oxytocin we need from human touch, and we do not feel valued from watching screens — in fact, scrolling through screens has the opposite effect.

All this technology is creating less connection. How often have you spent time with someone but felt like they were somewhere else in their thoughts and actions — perhaps texting or on their mobile phone, or generally just not being present with you? What impact did this have on you and the quality of the relationship? Have you been spending time with someone when suddenly their phone rings and they ask you if you mind if they answer? No doubt, you said it was fine, but is it really? How did you feel when that person answered the phone call mid-conversation? Doing so sends us a message that we are not valued. This would be okay if it just happened occasionally, but it happens all the time! You've likely also done these things yourself.

So my challenge to you is to stop, think and create a new pattern. Make an effort now to be truly present with others, to actively listen and to give them 100 per cent while you are together. If my phone goes off, I just leave it or, better still, I put it on silent. I've realised I'm not saving time, by taking the call straightaway. I'm just splitting my attention.

Truly being present and living in the moment takes conscious effort and self-discipline; however, it is well worth it. You will see your relationships transform if you focus on being truly present when you are together. Try having mealtimes together and turning off your phone and TV. Spend quality time together, connecting eye to eye, and heart to heart. Leave your device in the car or on silent out of sight when spending time with family and friends. Truly connecting makes a world of difference. When others feel valued, they will show how they value you too.

Connecting to improve wellbeing

Connection in your life is vital—not only with yourself but with everyone else around you. The quality of your interactions and connections can have a lasting influence on you and others. When we experience touch, connection and trust from others, our bodies produce oxytocin (commonly known as a hug hormone).

Quality social connections improve your wellbeing by:

- creating a positive feedback loop of social, emotional and physical wellbeing
- lowering levels of anxiety and depression
- increasing your self-esteem and empathy
- improving your happiness.

Let's take one last look at the findings of the Harvard study mentioned earlier in this chapter. In *Triumphs of Experience: The Men of the Harvard Grant Study*, study director George Vaillant (2012) examines the findings on what makes people happy. These included:

- The warmth of relationships throughout life has the greatest positive effect on life satisfaction.
- A sense of belonging leads to looking after yourself and others better.
- Happiness is love.

TAKING ACTION

Work on the quality of your connections to improve your own life, and the lives of those around you — including your family and your team.

CONNECTION ACTIVITIES

At work:

- Start meetings with a personal check-in, and ask how colleagues are feeling beyond work tasks.

- Designate 'tech-free zones' for face-to-face conversations without screens.

- Host walking or outdoor meetings to encourage both movement and deeper discussions.

- Encourage 'gratitude sharing' by starting or ending meetings with appreciation for team members.

- Introduce five-minute 'connection breaks' of casual chats or laughter breaks during the day.

- Pair employees as 'work buddies' to encourage support and accountability.

- Schedule team outdoor activities such as hikes, gardening or community clean-ups to foster bonding.

- Celebrate personal and team milestones, and recognise both work and life achievements.

- Encourage deeper questions in casual conversations and go beyond 'How are you?'

(continued)

- Have shared meals together to strengthen team connections.

At home:

- Implement 'no phone meal times' to prioritise uninterrupted conversation during meals.

- Schedule 'quality time windows' of dedicated time for one-on-one connection.

- Start a weekly 'walk and talk' tradition of strolling with family or friends while talking.

- Create a family or friend gratitude circle where you can share things you appreciate about each other.

- Engage in a shared hobby such as cooking, gardening or creative activities to foster deeper bonds.

- Host a 'tech-free evening' without screens.

- Surprise loved ones with small acts of kindness, such as a handwritten note or a thoughtful gesture.

- Use active listening in conversations through making eye contact and avoiding distractions.

- Do nature-based activities together, such as picnics, hiking, or simply watching the sunset.

TIME FOR ACTION QUESTIONS

- Who are the most important people to you in your life?

- Do you feel connected with these people?

- What could you do to create more quality connections?

- When was the last time you let them know that you are grateful they are in your life?

LET'S MAKE IT HAPPEN!

What can you do today to let someone close to you know how much you value them? Lock it in and make it happen!

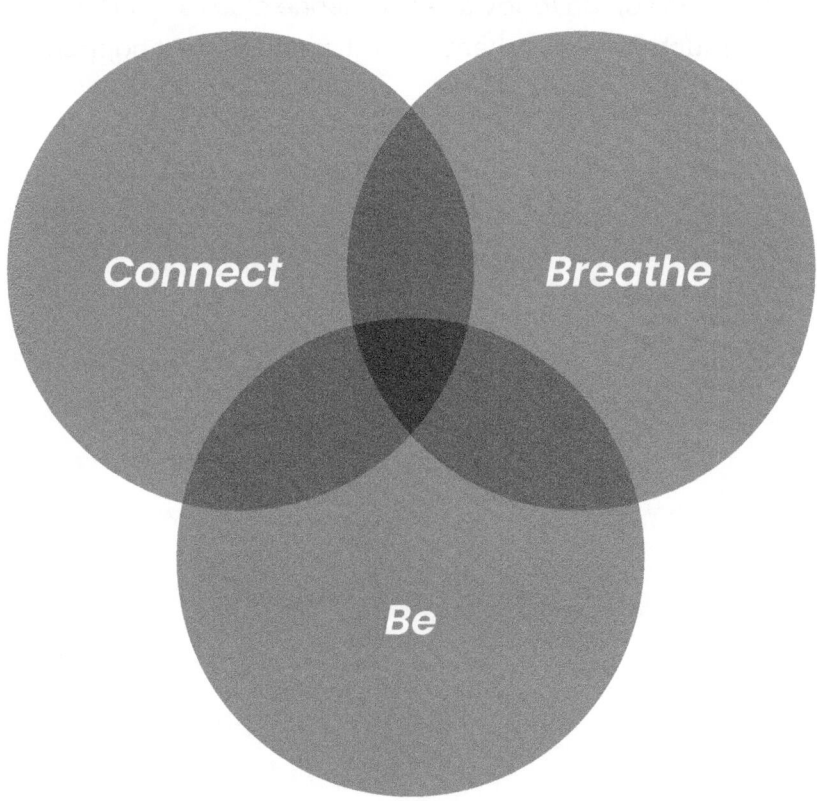

Elements in the breath GreenX7 tool

Chapter 17

Breath

I was in my mid-20s when I first truly discovered the power of breathing techniques — through a tall, lean, athletic Israeli called Erez Beatus. Erez, who had the ability to hold his breath for over eight minutes underwater, established the Israeli Freediving team and captained them through four world championships. When we first met, I was heavily into scuba diving and had 'blown bubbles' through thousands of dives. However, as Erez retold stories of holding his breath, gliding down into the deep blue waters and feeling at one with the ocean, I knew straightaway I had to try it.

I became good friends with Erez and his partner, Ally, bonding over the ocean and its marine life. When Erez introduced me to his breath-holding technique, I became addicted to not only freediving but also being able to use my breath to create a state of calm wherever I was — including on land.

While the *act* of freediving is to hold your breath underwater, the *art* of freediving, for me, is to be at one with the ocean, creating a state in mind and body that feels almost euphoric and Zen-like. People have told me that going deep into meditation can put you into a state of transcendence, and I have also felt the same when freediving — a feeling of pure bliss that is outside of the physical body.

Being present through breath

When I started learning to control my breath, I was still using boxing as a tool to reduce my frustrations. I loved it, but the problem was a bag wasn't always just hanging around when you needed it. What I love about breathing as a tool is that it's available 24/7.

Typically, your breath is part of the 'automatic' processes controlled by your medulla oblongata (which connects your brain to your spinal cord. You don't have to think about, and your body just does it automatically. However, by bringing attention to the breath, you can use it as a tool to reduce stress, be more conscious of your surroundings and help live in the moment.

When you take slow, gentle, deep breaths, your brain sends a message to your body to relax, lower your heart rate, and reduce muscle tension and anxiety. Studies have shown that using slow breathing practices, including slowing your breath to about six breaths per minute, can lead to significant physiological changed in just a few breaths.[48] I love how something so simple can create massive change.

Countless breathing techniques are available, with many being rooted in Eastern philosophy, and, over the years, I've explored a variety of these mindfulness and meditation practices. Through trial and experience, I've discovered a simple yet highly effective approach that works for me — breathing in for five seconds, pausing briefly, and then exhaling for five seconds. Interestingly, this is the same technique taught in scuba diving to regulate and slow breathing, helping to conserve air and maintain a calm, steady rhythm.

In his 2020 book *Breath: The New Science of a Lost Art*, science journalist James Nestor concludes that the optimum breathing rate is 5.5 breaths per minute — which equates to 5.5-second inhales and 5.5-second exhales, in and out through your nose. Motivational speaker and extreme athlete Wim Hof has created a cult following based on his specialised breathing techniques (and using this in connection with cold therapy, such as ice baths or cold showers). Personally, from my own practice and trying to make it sustainable in my own life, I keep it simple. I use slow, deep breathing in through my nose and out through my nose whenever I feel the need to slow down or calm down, or just want to be 100 per cent present in the moment. I would typically do this for 10 breaths, with my eyes closed, my bare feet on the earth, and feeling my stomach and chest rise as I breathe in and out. Before learning to breathe for stress relief, I would clench my fists — now I release them.

When we focus on our breath, we reconnect back to ourselves, and we become present. We are so good at *doing* that we rarely give ourselves permission to stop and just *be*. We spend a lot of our day on autopilot, and when we allow ourselves a moment to breathe, we come into the moment. I love doing a breath session in our workshops and watching people's minds and bodies relax, slow down and cheer up with an upward curl of their mouth.

Sometimes even now I struggle being present. I can see when Carly and I are out on our morning walks and I'm stuck in my head, the connection between us suffers. When I am present, I am happy and fun, we play and muck around. However, when I am stuck in my head, I just walk silently, not seeing, not taking in the beauty — I am there but not present. The day just doesn't start off as well. In these moments, I really must make a deliberate effort to focus on my breath, bringing myself back to the present moment so I can enjoy those precious moments.

Using breath to improve wellbeing

Deep breathing offers numerous benefits that can enhance your overall wellbeing. Engaging in deep breathing techniques can lead to the release of neurochemicals, including endorphins, which promote a sense of wellbeing and can alleviate pain. Additionally, deep breathing activates your body's relaxation response, reducing stress and anxiety levels.

By consciously practising deep breathing, you can experience several positive outcomes, such as:

- *Reduced pain:* Deep breathing has been shown to alleviate pain by promoting relaxation and reducing muscle tension.
- *Elevated mood:* Engaging in deep breathing exercises can enhance mood and overall emotional wellbeing.
- *Improved lymphatic system function:* Deep breathing stimulates the lymphatic system, aiding in the removal of toxins and supporting immune function.
- *Enhanced cardiovascular capacity:* Regular practice of deep breathing can improve cardiovascular health by lowering blood pressure and heart rate.
- *Better stress and anxiety management:* Deep breathing activates the parasympathetic nervous system, promoting relaxation and reducing stress and anxiety.
- *Improved mental clarity:* Practising deep breathing can enhance focus and cognitive function.
- *Increased energy levels:* Deep breathing techniques can boost energy by improving oxygen exchange and circulation.

- *Enhanced sleep quality:* Incorporating deep breathing into your routine can improve sleep by promoting relaxation.

- *Reconnection with the body:* Deep breathing fosters a stronger mind–body connection, enhancing bodily awareness and mindfulness.[49]

TAKING ACTION

Your breath is a remarkable built-in tool—always with you, effortlessly accessible and completely free to use whenever you need it.

BREATH ACTIVITIES

At work:

- Begin each workday with three mindful breaths, as you set an intention to stay present.

- Use a 'breath pause' of one deep inhale and exhale to reset focus before meetings.

- Practise the '5-5-5 grounding breath': inhale for five counts, hold for five, exhale for five before important tasks.

- Breathe before answering emails or calls to create a space for a more mindful response.

- Incorporate breath awareness into task switching by taking one slow breath before moving to the next task.

- Take a 'silent breath break' before presentations to help reduce nerves and improve clarity. Encourage any members of your team presenting with you to do the same.

(continued)

- Use breath to stay present and engaged in conversations by inhaling deeply when listening.

- Pair breath with walking, focusing on deep, rhythmic breaths to stay present while moving.

- Create a 'breath to focus' ritual, such as three breaths before deep work sessions to sharpen concentration.

- Exhale stress before leaving work to help you shift from work mode to home presence.

At home:

- Take three deep breaths before stepping into your home to help transition mindfully from work to family time.

- Use breath to set an intention for presence — for example, inhale clarity, exhale distractions before engaging with loved ones.

- Pause and breathe before responding in conversations to encourage thoughtful, present communication.

- Sync deep breathing with everyday moments, such as while drinking tea, cooking or folding laundry.

- Try 'sunrise breathing' outdoors — inhale slowly while watching the sun rise to start the day grounded.

- Use bedtime breathwork to unwind, by using slow exhales to release tension before sleep.

- Practise breath gratitude — for example, inhale appreciation, exhale worry while reflecting on the day.

- Step outside and take a nature breath pause, closing your eyes and taking three full breaths to feel connected.

- Take a deep, mindful breath before family meals to be fully present before eating.

TIME FOR ACTION QUESTIONS

- What places or environments inspire you to be more present?

- What breathing practices have you tried or found helpful? If you haven't found any, could you look for a meditation class, yoga class or app to try — for example, Headspace (www.headspace.com) or Calm (www.calm.com/app)?

- What time of day would be good for you to practise breathing?

LET'S MAKE IT HAPPEN!

Try to focus on your breath for a few minutes today when you feel anxious or overwhelmed. Try the following to stop, connect and breathe:

- Breathe in and out slowly, gently and deeply through your nose.

- If thoughts come in, focus back on your breathing. Tell yourself, 'Now I am breathing in through my nose. Now I am breathing out through my nose.'

- Try to achieve 10 long, slow, deep breaths in and out through your nose.

- Allow yourself to relax and be present, and enjoy the moment of reconnecting to your breath.

- Now close your eyes and breathe.

See if you feel any calmer afterwards. Encourage a similar practice for everyone on your team.

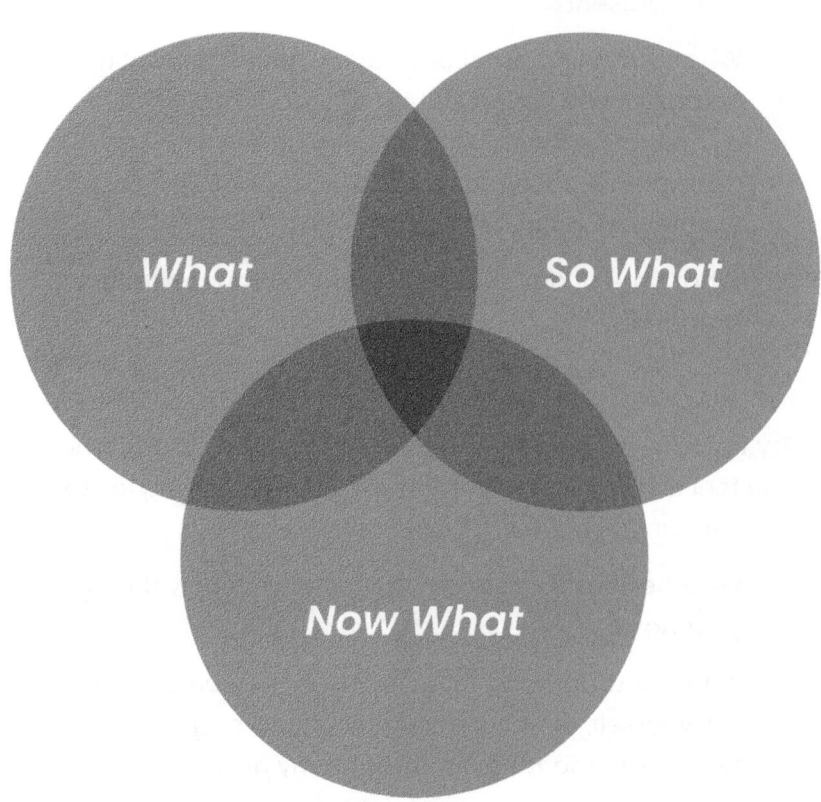

Elements of the reflection GreenX7 tool

Chapter 18
Reflection

You don't know what you don't know. That's what I know now and, to be honest, each year and decade that go by I look back and shake my head and say, 'Geez, kid — what the hell were you on about?!' But that's the beauty of growing into what is hopefully a better version of you each week, year and decade that passes.

At the ripe age of 43, I'm definitely not ready to dust off my hands, put my feet up and call it a day on trying to be the best version of myself. And I don't imagine I ever will be. I'm too intrigued to see where I can get to, to understand my full capacity as a human being and to reach my fullest potential — whatever that may be. When I do reflect on how I've grown mentally, emotionally and physically in just this past decade, it makes my heart swell with pride. I'm happier, healthier and just overall a better human being to others through opening up my heart and allowing love and life to join me on this journey. Venturing into the unknown is exciting, knowing (at least) that it can only be for the positive.

I think the hardest part of my work is seeing people who are stuck and not open to change, even when they know that their life is crumbling around them because of their stubbornness and conviction to remain steadfast. My dad's generation came from a time when toughness was the default setting — when the 'school of hard knocks' was worn like a badge of honour. Many of them were taught to push through pain, stay silent and carry on no matter what. And, even now, as some face serious health challenges — both physical and mental — that old mindset can still be hard to shake. But here's the thing: looking after your health isn't just about you. It's also about the people who love you. That kind of toughness shaped the men of my father's generation, but it also came at a cost. Many still carry their pain in silence, believing they're too strong to fall — until they do. And when that happens, the impact ripples outward. It's not just their struggle. It's their partners, their children and their mates who are left to hold the weight. Choosing to take care of yourself isn't weakness — it's responsibility.

But, again, this is also a case of you don't know what you don't know — unless, of course, someone is literally hitting you over the head with it time and time again and you are still not open to listening. Looking after yourself isn't just about you; it's also about how it will have a positive impact on those around you.

It reminds me of a joke my dad tells. A man falls out of his sailing boat and is floating out at sea. As he is praying to God to save his life, a ship passes and the captain asks if he needs help. He tells them to keep going because God will save him. After a few more ships offer the same assistance and he again turns them down, saying that God will save him, he finally runs out of energy and drowns. When he gets to heaven and sees God he asks, 'Why did you not save me God?'

God replies, 'I tried — I sent four ships to your rescue'.

What I've learned is that you need to be open to growth and change — and grabbing the lifelines that are thrown your way. Looking after yourself is not selfish but the opposite. The more you look after yourself, the less others have to look after you and the more you can look after others. It's simple if you reflect on it.

Reflecting on your wellbeing

Reflection invites you to take the time to reflect on and bring positive change to specific areas in your life. Giving yourself permission to explore personal experiences, feelings and events means you can reconsider these from a fresh perspective. Your life is like a puzzle — the components are all interlinked, and one missing or out of balance part affects the whole.

Sometimes you might feel that you're not as happy or healthy as you would like, but working out what the actual issue is can be hard work. Reflection gives you the opportunity to understand yourself more clearly so you can maximise your strengths and work on your challenges. What I like to call 'miss-takes' (rather than 'mistakes') can be a wonderful opportunity for learning and personal growth if you take the time to reflect. All change begins with you firstly becoming more aware of yourself and the situations you are facing. If you live in denial, no change is possible. The benefits that come from reflection then support you to better understand your emotions, strengths, weaknesses and impact on others, while also allowing you to appreciate where you are at, offering an opportunity to bring positive change to your everyday life.

Remember — working out a clear direction moving forward is difficult without taking the time to reflect on what and how you have come to be who and where you are at today.

In any reflective practice having areas to bring focus to will provide the most value. You can explore how you are living within each of these awareness areas, and how this may be affecting your overall wellbeing.

More specifically, reflection provides the following benefits:

- helping you gain insight and see how to move forward
- increasing your self-awareness and self-regulation
- prioritising and creating space for self-care
- increasing awareness of life priorities.

TAKING ACTION

Take some time today to reflect on and bring positive change to specific areas in your life, including at work and with your team.

REFLECTION ACTIVITIES

At work:

- At the end of each workday, reflect on your wins and write down three things you accomplished.

- Before starting work each morning, reflect on your top priority and set an intention for the day.

- At the end of each week, reflect on successes, challenges, and areas for improvement.

- Take a moment to pause and reflect before mindfully switching tasks.

- Start a work gratitude journal and write down one thing each day that you appreciate about your job or team.

- After important meetings, reflect on and note key takeaways and how you can implement them. Discuss these with your team and ask for their reflections.

- Rather than seeing mistakes as 'failure', reflect on them with a growth mindset by noting what was learned. Again, discuss these learnings with your team.

- Complete a 'self check-in' through the day, asking yourself, 'How am I feeling?' and 'What do I need to adjust?'

- Reflect on workplace interactions, and consider how you engaged with others and how to improve relationships.

- When facing a challenge, try a creative problem-solving reflection and write out potential solutions before acting.

At home:

- Take five minutes before bed for an evening reflection, thinking about your day's highlights.

(continued)

- List three things you're grateful for every day.

- Each Sunday, reflect on the past week and plan positive habits for the upcoming week.

- Take a moment for mindful breathing and reflection, by taking a deep breath and recalling a moment of joy from the day.

- Take some family reflection time at dinner — discussing, for example, 'What was the best part of your day?'

- Write responses in your journal to reflection prompts such as 'What made me happy today?'

- Spend time in nature and mentally reflect on and review your thoughts, emotions and goals.

- Perform a monthly personal growth check-in, reflecting on personal goals, habits and progress.

- Use an emotional awareness reflection to identify and process emotions before reacting to stressful situations.

- Reflect with self-compassion to think about moments where you were hard on yourself and reframe them with kindness.

TIME FOR ACTION QUESTIONS

Think about an area or situation in your life that you feel needs your attention and ask yourself the following questions.

What?

- Describe the event, experience, or situation.

- Focus on facts and observations.

- For example, what happened? What was my role? What did I notice?

So what?

- Explore the meaning and significance of the experience.

- Analyse emotions, challenges and learning outcomes.

- For example, why does this matter? What did I learn? How did this impact me or others?

Now what?

- Focus on applying the learning to future actions or decisions.

- Encourage your own personal growth and practical change.

- For example, what will I do differently next time? How can I use this experience moving forward?

LET'S MAKE IT HAPPEN!

What do you do to reflect on your day-to-day journey? What could you do? What is one area of your life that you want to bring focus to and how could you improve this? Make it happen!

CASE STUDY: REFLECTING TO RECHARGE

Sarah is an amazing woman. She is a high achiever, and a wonderful mother, daughter and wife. She always looks good and has lots of friends. Everyone wonders how she does it all. A big part of the answer is that Sarah takes time to reflect on what she needs, and then makes sure she takes care of herself.

A recent weekend provides an excellent example of this. The weekend had been busy for Sarah. The kids had had their sports activities, Sarah had planned and hosted a 70th birthday party for her mother, and she'd managed to finish off an important work project while the kids were watching some TV. Although she was tired, she was satisfied with what she had achieved on the weekend. Then, on Sunday lunchtime, one of her children came down with a stomach virus. Sarah had an important work presentation on Monday, and could see that on top of her busy weekend she was now going to get no sleep while she cared for her sick children. She could see her battery was going to be very low on Monday, and that it was going to be very difficult for her to deliver a quality presentation and make it through the week at work.

Sarah had two options here: soldier on with a low battery and risk burnout and delivering a below par presentation, or use the GreenX7 app to get an overview of what areas of her life were out of balance and use the tools to get her battery energy recharged.

Luckily Sarah remembered to use the app and could see that getting extra sleep and focusing on her physical health was going to be critical for her. She shared her GreenX7 app results with her husband and discussed how important the presentation on Monday was for her career. They agreed that she could take some time off on Sunday afternoon to go for a walk near the beach and then come home and take a nap. They decided to take turns to care for the children through the night and, in the morning, she started the day with her recharge morning routine — a smoothie, meditation and yoga. This helped Sarah to recharge enough to deliver her presentation to the standard she knew she was capable.

PART IV

PULLING IT ALL TOGETHER

Modern life doesn't ever seem to slow down, and we all can constantly feel like we're being pulled in different directions by distractions, deadlines and endless to-do lists. In the noise, it's easy to lose sight of ourselves — our needs, our energy, our joy. This is where the real power of the GreenX7 tools come in.

On its own, each tool is valuable. But when combined into a daily rhythm, something powerful happens. You stop reacting, and start realigning. You move through your day with more intention, more presence and more flow. Some people call this a routine — but I like to think of it as a rhythm. A rhythm that moves with you, adapts to you and brings you back to what matters.

This part of the book is where it all comes together. I show you how to combine the GreenX7 tools to create a seamless rhythm that saves time, restores energy and builds real momentum. You'll start to see how the awareness areas are deeply connected — and how small, thoughtful actions can have ripple effects across your whole life.

And your focus becomes not just about what you do, but also about how you connect and how you show up each and every day. In this part, I also guide you through using the Play for Your Life cards — which provide a powerful tool to spark the kind of conversations that create true change — conversations with yourself, and with the people you care about, creating true connections.

Finally, I ask you the most important question of all: *How full is your battery?* Because everything — your energy, your relationships and your performance — flows from that answer.

Chapter 19

Finding your rhythm

Using the GreenX7 tools means you can create a rhythm that will help your everyday wellness. Yes, you can use them individually but I know you're likely time-poor, impatient and just want quick wins. So, I'm going to give you a life hack on how you can combine the GreenX7 tools into one or two daily activities, so you have no excuse not to complete these activities and grow into the best version of yourself.

I'll start off by giving you my life rhythm; it's what I use each day and helps me reconnect to myself, others and nature for my own everyday wellness. Some days I miss out — perhaps because I'm travelling or facilitating early gigs. However, make no mistake, this is my priority, and I do my best to always incorporate this rhythm because of its positive impact on my wellbeing and the connection it builds with those in my life, both personally and professionally.

After you've read my rhythm, you can create your own based on your own circumstances.

My daily wellness rhythm

For me, being able to thrive sustainably is the most important thing that I can do, not only for myself but also for those around me. I don't want to just survive through life — I want to thrive! As far as I know, I've only got one life, so I really want to be the best version I can be. And I don't mean just on a weekend or on a holiday — I mean every single day.

Before getting into my daily rhythm, let's rewind to many moons ago, when I didn't think about my own wellbeing as something I had control over. I didn't understand that you could create a rhythm and take control of your own life. Back then, life controlled me. I didn't understand that I could do things to improve myself on a daily basis. Life just happened to me. Some days were good, some days were bad, and some days were really bad. I thought that was just how life was. I didn't know how to create a life that supported me rather than one that I needed to support.

As I outline in chapter 1, a lot of things happened in my life that inspired me to make a change. I needed to flick the switch for me to want to be the best version of myself. I needed a *why*. If you don't have a strong enough 'why', you probably won't be able to sustain a daily rhythm. The sustaining piece is the hardest part, of course, but it's also the most rewarding.

I find the easiest way to create a daily rhythm is to start with your sleep. Sleep really is the foundation of wellbeing; you need to have the energy to take care of yourself, and that means trying to get between seven and eight hours of good quality sleep. (I know — this is coming from the author who has two kids under four!)

To give myself the best chance, I make sure to switch off all technology by 8.30 pm. When I go to bed, I then spend around 30 minutes reading or connecting with Carly until lights out. This gives my body a chance to get ready for sleep and for my natural melatonin to kick in. In modern life, with artificial lighting and technology, our bodies can find it hard to wind-down at the end of the day, so making sure you give your body trigger points for bedtime is important.

I wake up at around 4.30 am. (Don't worry — I'm not expecting you to do the same, unless that's what also works for you.) Since I wake up at the same time every day, my body is usually ready to get up and go. Before I created my daily rhythm, I was hitting the snooze button again and again. Rolling out of bed was always a hard slog, usually accompanied by the thought, *Oh no, not another day!* These days, I am happy to wake up in the morning because I really enjoy my rhythm. Well, as long as Sonny and Frankie have not kept me up all night!

I like waking up early because I perform best in the mornings and having these early hours allows me to prepare for my day without distractions. While I'm a morning person, you might be more of a night owl and dislike early mornings. You must follow what suits you individually.

Once awake, I head out to our home studio and prime my body and brain for the day with some stretches, callisthenics, and a sprinkling of mindfulness and gratitude. By doing this, I am looking after my physical and mental health, and creating a positive change in my body by releasing serotonin. I then make myself a coffee and sit down to read to further engage my brain and knowledge in whatever endeavour I'm currently immersing myself in.

Right now, I have three books on my coffee table that I'm reading, depending on what I'm working on. The first is *Bird by Bird: Instructions on Writing and Life* by Anne Lamott, which is giving me some guidance on writing this book. The next is *Conscious Leadership: Elevating Humanity Through Leadership* by Whole Foods co-founder John Mackey (and his co-authors). I coach leaders who are making an impact within and outside of their organisations, so any knowledge I can get on this subject is invaluable. And the third is *Start with Why: How Great Leaders Inspire Everyone to Take Action*, the Simon Sinek classic, which I am constantly picking up. I enjoy working with companies to help marry up their organisational values and reflect this to future employees, so they find the right candidates not just at an academic or skills level but also at a values-based level. I guess this process can be similar to finding the right romantic partner. They may look good on paper or in person, but you also must gel and have similar values and beliefs; otherwise, the relationship could go sour when the big discussions pop up.

By around 5.00 am, I'm getting stuck into the most important task of the day without the distractions of the world. At around 6.30 am, I head into the house and greet my three favourite people. This is one of my most cherished times of the day because, right in front of me, are the very reasons I want to be the best version of myself. It's a wonderful confirmation and it also creates a beautiful positive connection with my family. I'm lucky that Carly and I work off the same body clock. (Although I have to admit she is losing a lot more sleep than I am at the moment. Sorry love!)

At around 7.00 am, we ride to Kingscliff beach, go for a 30-minute walk, and then pull up stumps at a local, grab coffees and spend some quality time connecting with our community in between swims at the beach or creek. This can change depending on the season.

Within those few hours in the morning, I've done everything that I need to do for my mental, emotional and physical health. I've ticked off all of my GreenX7 tools, and enjoyed a perfect morning of reconnecting to self, others and nature for everyday wellness. No matter what happens from that point on, I already feel like I have seized the day.

To sum up, my rhythm for Monday to Friday is as follows:

- *8.30 pm:* Switch off all technology.
- *8.30–9.00 pm:* Connect with Carly and/or read a fiction book.
- *9.00 pm:* Lights out.
- *4.30 am:* Wake up.
- *4.30–5.00 am:* Stretches, mindfulness, coffee and book.
- *5.00–6.30 am:* Work on the most urgent and important tasks, while not being interrupted.
- *7.00–8.30 am:* Adams family adventure.
- *8.30 am:* Ready to seize the day, whatever may come.

During the day, I try to get some bonus wellbeing points. If I'm working in the city with a park nearby, I'll grab something healthy to eat for lunch, take off my shoes and sit under a tree while I eat, enjoying the natural surroundings. If I'm working from home, I'll just head out into the backyard and do the same thing. If I've had a productive morning, I might allow myself one or two hours throughout the day to have some fun. Basically, I'll add in anything that gets me ticking off the GreenX7 tools. So that's what a rhythm is — it's about creating something that you can do each and every day and looking for ways to tick off the tools.

In the next section, I run through some activities that combine many of the tools into one activity to amplify the wellbeing benefits.

Setting your daily rhythm with GreenX7 activities

Here's how to set your daily rhythm and add more GreenX7 tools to your day, starting with your morning routine:

- Wake up and step outside, barefoot, for five minutes of deep breathing and earthing.

- Engage in light stretching or exercise outdoors while focusing on your breath.

- Set a daily intention and reflect on one thing you're grateful for.

- Eat breakfast mindfully, free from screens, and engage in a short conversation.

- If commuting, choose an active option such as walking or cycling, or spend a few minutes outside before work.

Work routine:

- Begin the workday with three deep breaths as you set your top three priorities.

- Take a short stretch or movement break every hour, stepping outside if possible.

- Opt for a walking or standing meeting to integrate movement and focus.

- Use mid-morning breaks for deep breathing and a quick nature moment.
- Step outside for fresh air and sunlight after lunch, preferably barefoot.

Midday recharge:

- Take a minute for deep breathing before starting afternoon tasks.
- Walk outside, stretch in the sun, or do grounding exercises for five minutes.
- Check in on your energy levels (and those of your team) and adjust pace accordingly.
- Step away from work for a mindful hydration break, breathing deeply.

End of workday:

- Reflect on three accomplishments and one lesson from the day.
- Engage in a movement-based activity, such as a walk, run or outdoor play.
- Eat dinner outside or in a relaxed space while focusing on the conversation.

Evening wind-down:

- Take a short walk at sunset, practising deep breathing and reflection.
- Spend time with family or friends in a tech-free environment.
- Engage in light stretching or relaxation exercises before bed.

- Reflect on a joyful moment from the day and set an intention for tomorrow.

- Ensure a dark, quiet and tech-free sleep environment.

Once you have your daily rhythm working for you, you can start to set an example for those around you, including your team and those you lead.

Remember — you can mix your daily rhythm up depending on your work and family situation, but the main thing to remember is do something each day. I've also found that if the activity is too hard or not enjoyable, it won't be sustainable. Keep it fun, and mix it up based on how your day is looking. If you're travelling for work, for example, use your maps app to see what you can create in your location. Make it a challenge and see how many GreenX7 tools you can tick off.

My rhythm could be completely different to how yours ends up looking, but the important thing to remember is to make it work for you around your current situation.

Now it's your turn. Go through each tool and write down how you can combine them together. To help you get started, I've provided an example in the following worksheet.

Make your daily rhythm work for you and remember — if it's fun, it will get done.

 Go for a **30-minute walk** at a steady, mindful pace. Let your body move freely and naturally.

 Choose a natural outdoor setting — a park, trail, beach or bush track. Let your senses connect with the space around you.

 Walk barefoot for part of your time, or sit/stand on natural ground for at least **20 minutes** to allow your system to ground and regulate.

 Keep the experience phone-free and distraction-free. Protect this time — no multitasking, just being present.

 Bring someone with you. Walk and talk with intention, or share quiet presence together. If alone, connect with yourself through mindful awareness.

 While walking or resting, practice deep, rhythmic breathing. Inhale through the nose, exhale longer through the mouth. Use breath to stay centred.

 End your walk with a few minutes sitting in nature. Reflect or journal: What do I feel now? What shifted? What do I need more of today?

Combining the GreenX7 tools to create your daily rhythm — nature walk example

Connecting the GreenX7 tools to your battery

The brilliance of the GreenX7 tools (from part III) and eight wellness areas that form your battery (from part II) lies in their seamless synergy. Together, they form a system designed to not just sustain you, but also help you thrive. Each tool plays a vital role, but it's their connection to one another that makes them truly transformative. Movement generates energy, for example, but it's the right environment that sustains it. Breath calms the mind, but it's reflection that brings clarity and direction. Connection nurtures relationships, but it's only with time that we can truly invest in them.

This isn't about quick fixes or working on just one area of life — it's about understanding that wellbeing is a rhythm, and a dynamic flow of energy that requires balance. Your personal battery powers everything you do, from your health and mindset to your relationships and ability to experience joy. But energy isn't limitless. Without the right tools to recharge, you drift into survival mode, running on empty instead of thriving.

What also makes this framework so powerful is its simplicity. It doesn't demand drastic change; only a realignment with what already exists within you. When you integrate these tools into your daily life, they become second nature, and lay a foundation for resilience, clarity and deep fulfilment. You're no longer just focused on getting through the day, and can create a life in which you are fully present, fully engaged and fully energised.

The GreenX7 tools all play a role in maintaining and recharging your personal battery, but some tools carry more weight in certain areas than others. While each one contributes to overall wellbeing, some tools have a more direct and powerful impact on specific battery areas, while others serve as supporting elements that enhance or sustain progress.

Movement, for example, is a driving force behind physical health, energy, fun and sleep, keeping the body strong and resilient. Environment shapes your daily habits, influencing sleep quality, nutrition and mindset by creating spaces that either support or hinder wellbeing. Earthing helps regulate energy, reduces stress and strengthens the immune system, providing the body with a natural way to recharge. Time plays a critical role in balancing priorities, ensuring that you invest in the areas of life that matter most — health, fun, relationships and self-care. Connection is fundamental to emotional resilience, strengthening friendships and relationships while also impacting mindset and overall happiness. Breath acts as a powerful regulator, calming the nervous system, improving focus and maintaining steady energy levels. Finally, reflection ties everything together, allowing you to process experiences, gain clarity and realign with your purpose.

Some tools act as catalysts while others maintain balance, but none work in isolation. The beauty of this framework is in its synergy — when all seven tools are used together, they create a complete and self-sustaining system for wellbeing. Just as a battery needs different components to function efficiently, your energy and resilience depend on the careful balance of movement, environment, earthing, time, connection, breath and reflection.

Even if one tool plays a bigger role in a certain area, the combination of all seven is what creates lasting impact. So don't rely on just one tool, but integrate all seven in a way that supports a sustainable, thriving life.

SIDE STORY: THE SHAMAN

Perhaps you remember a certain stage in your life that made you stop and scratch your head. Perhaps you wondered whether you were on the right path, or doing what you should be doing. Perhaps you asked yourself, 'How do I know who I really am?' We might call these existential crises.

After a long-term relationship ended, I found myself somewhere in the middle of a midlife meltdown and an existential crisis. I was in my mid 30s at the time, and everything I had envisioned had come to fruition. I lived in paradise, I owned my own home, I was healthy and happy, had great friends and family, and successful businesses.

But the one thing that I really wanted and desired had not eventuated, and that was to be a father.

I was worried that I wasn't going to find the right girl, settle down and have a family. (I had the Cat Stevens song 'Father and Son' playing on repeat in my head.)

Becoming a dad has always been important to me. I needed to know that I could be a good one. I needed to know that I could teach my child all the things that I wish I had been taught when growing up. I also wanted to relive my childhood, and those memories of someone teaching me to fish, surf, camp and even shave. I wanted to feel what it would be like to take the time to teach, learn and discover what it is to be a man. I wanted to go through the initiation from boy to manhood. So many of these things I missed out on when growing up, and I wanted to relive them through a child of my own. I wanted a family.

I thought that having a family would make me feel at home, at peace, and grounded — that a family would stop me from constantly wondering and wandering. I thought a family would be the final piece of the puzzle and I could finally stop searching.

While in the midst of this crisis, I had a conversation with my friend Matt, who had just come back from an existential journey of his own — in his case, on a weekend retreat in a tepee lead by a female shaman. He told me a story about his own epiphany, and finding answers to what he was questioning in his own life, and he told me he had found those answers inside that tepee.

Normally, I wouldn't be open to such alternative methods, but I was on a year of discovery, and I knew that I had something that needed discovering — that piece of the puzzle, which I must have dropped on the floor and just couldn't find.

So, I took myself off to see the shaman. The first thing I noticed when she opened the door was her clear and brilliant blue eyes. They seemed to radiate from within, and gave me almost the same feeling as jumping into a pool of soul-refreshing goodness — the feeling you get when it's a scorching hot day and you dive into the cool ocean.

After a brief consultation, she led me into a room full of crystals and dream catchers, with oils evaporating into the air. She asked me to lie face up on a table, and placed an array of crystals and objects I didn't have a name for on me.

'Tim', she said as I closed my eyes. 'I'm going to ask you now to go into a dreamlike state. You will hear a drum beating slowly at first. When it's time to come out of your dream, you will hear the drum beating faster, until it stops and then it's time for you to come back.'

'Where am I going? What am I looking for?' I asked the shaman.

'You will know when you find it', she said.

As she started slowly beating the drum above my lower abdomen, I felt the vibrations through my body, and wondered what to do next.

I'm not sure how long I lay there, but suddenly I appeared in front of a giant waterfall. A huge mountain of rock lay before me, and I started to walk towards it. When I got closer, I could see through the mists of water a large opening behind the waterfall. I climbed up and into a cave, slowly finding my way to the back until I came across a large tree trunk that came up through the floor. I scrambled my way down the tree trunk and found myself in a beautiful forest that seemed to be glowing. Everywhere I looked, I could see butterflies fluttering about in all sizes and colours. As I peered to my left, a sparkling creek shimmered as the water bubbled away downstream.

I had no idea what I was looking for, so I started to follow the stream, taking in all the beauty around me. I felt like I was in a wonderland.

That's when I noticed a figure sitting on a large boulder in the middle of the stream, fishing. I walked on and watched his body grow larger; I remember I was at peace, with a feeling of total contentment. When I came alongside the figure, I jumped across the boulders to meet him in the middle of the stream and sat down next to him. I felt like a child being protected, and knew that I was safe and would always be safe. I looked up at him; a large brown, hairy face with a long snout and black eyes peered down at me. It was a grizzly bear.

With a broad smile he opened his mouth and said, 'Hello, Tim'.

'I am supposed to ask you a question', I said, 'but I don't know what to ask you.'

'Yes, you do. It's right there inside of you. You just have to ask', said the bear.

A moment of silence passed between us and then the question came to me. 'How do I know I've found home?'

'You are home, you're with me. I'm within you. And anytime you feel like you need to come home, you can meet me right here, sitting on this boulder.'

We sat on those boulders by the sparkling creek, watching the butterflies and taking in the beauty and serenity, and then I heard the drum beat grow louder and faster.

'I'll walk you back', said the bear.

We walked across the rocks and alongside the creek towards the big tree trunk, as the drums beat louder and faster. I asked, 'Why is the creek sparkling?'

'That's your soul, Tim.'

'Why are there so many butterflies?'

'They are all your ideas, Tim.'

We climbed the tree trunk into the cave and walked to the opening behind the sheath of water that cascaded to the pool below.

I could hear the drums so loud and clear; I knew that my time was up.

'If you ever need to come home, Tim, you know where to find me.'

The drums stopped, I opened my eyes, and I knew I was home. I was at peace.

As I was driving away in a state of euphoria, I reflected on my journey with the shaman, trying to piece together all that I felt, seen, heard and witnessed.

When I got to my literal home, I opened up my journal and wrote, 'Everything that we need is within us'.

Chapter 20

Opening up

When Mal took his life, I started to understand the significant difference between *communication* and *connection*. Mal and I were always adept at communicating with each other. We were mates and business partners, and we had to communicate, sometimes whether we liked it or not. When I think back, I realised I had always been an excellent communicator. I probably owe this to my parents, who are both very charismatic and can always make themselves heard. Even in primary school, I would get an A for my talks — apart from one time when I got a B+ because I was overconfident!

Mal was the same. He was an excellent communicator, orator and storyteller. Yet, now that I know the difference, we both could have been better at connecting — and not just with each other, but also with those around us.

Again, you don't know what you don't know and, really, I didn't know the difference between communicating and connecting, or even how to create a deeper connection. Growing up in a house full of boys, connection went out the window.

Having the courage to connect

So, what do I know now that I didn't then that could have potentially saved the life of another person? I have been following Brené Brown since starting my own wellbeing journey. The outgoing Texan who tells it how it is has been studying the courage of vulnerability for many years, and what I'm learning is that it takes bravery to connect, because to connect we have to be open and to be open we need to be vulnerable and this, my friends, takes courage!

For the majority of blokes, if given the choice they would probably rather run across burning hot coals or strap on boxing gloves than sit down and truthfully answer the question, 'How are you feeling?' Even if you have finally built up the courage or you've gotten to a point where you're about to flick the off switch, how do you synthesise all that white noise in your head, piece it together and explain to the person opposite you the many layers of why you feel like you're just surviving? No wonder when people ask whether we're okay, our typical response is, 'I'm fine'.

I was recently coaching a young woman who, to the outside world, seemed to have the world at her feet. She had a loving and supportive circle to embrace her, and endless opportunities. However, when we dug deeper, she admitted that in the previous week she had been considering taking her life because she didn't want to disappoint her dad. I made it very clear that her dad would be much more disappointed if, after she took her own life, he found a letter explaining why. The positive was that, during our session, she was willing to be open and I was willing to listen.

But, as we know, this isn't always the case. We lose so many of our friends, family and colleagues to suicide because parties on both sides aren't really connecting. They may have been communicating, but they're not necessarily connecting and, in doing so, creating that deeper conversation to discover the hidden truths.

In chapter 1, I mention that after Mal took his life, I needed to find a way to help not just men but everyone as well to open up and create deeper conversations. My whole life up to that point was based on exterior toughness, but never did I think of flexing my internal toughness to be vulnerable. This was where our Play for Your Life cards came in. Sometimes, I still struggle to this day, and find myself playing the cards just to unravel all the thoughts in my mind and make sense of where I am and what I need to do to move forward in a positive direction. What I have learned along the way is that by playing the cards you can create the time and space for another person (or yourself) to think about and understand you and the world around you.

Through actively listening and connecting, you also create a sense of feeling valued in the other person. One of the most important discoveries I have learned along this journey of mine is that feeling valued creates self-worth for ourselves and others, which in turn creates self-love. I believe that each day we need to make a deliberate effort to create value, meaning and belonging in our lives and the lives of others so we can make ourselves and others feel worthy of the life we are living.

Here's a refresher on what those three things mean:

- *Value:* To feel like you are being valued and valuing others.
- *Meaning:* To have a sense of purpose in this life.
- *Belonging:* To feel like you belong to a tribe.

When I coach individuals using the GreenX7 tools, I'm helping them create a daily rhythm that includes points of contact throughout the day. Combined, this rhythm creates value, meaning and belonging, so each night, consciously and subconsciously, that person has the self-worth to feel deserving of care, and to want to continue the positive cycle of being open and embracing connection over communication.

In chapter 16, I mention the Harvard Study of Adult Development (previously known as the Grant Study). I first came across this study back in 2015, when I was trying to understand why Mal took his life. What I learned led me on a path that diverged from the normal realms of wellbeing, which even to this day are still focused too narrowly on physical health, nutrition and mindfulness. I also mention in chapter 16 that the study findings highlighted something exceeded these aspects for a predictor of life satisfaction and, more surprisingly, had a bigger impact on your health and happiness. And that something was a history of warm, intimate relationships. As George Vaillant, who directed the study for more than three decades, concluded 'Happiness equals love — full stop'.[50]

This might not be what you expected. It certainly wasn't what I expected, but it seems that warmth of your relationships — that is, the warmth of your connections — is the greatest indicator for life satisfaction.

Finding the tools to open up

As I've looked back through the many chapters of my life, I've realised that being open can be both an innate and a learned skill. When I was a kid, I was always so happy and open, and the environment around me nurtured having emotions, feelings and a sense of being free to express my inner feelings without even thinking about there being consequences. I didn't need a filter as to what I should and shouldn't say, and I didn't contemplate whether this was a good time to cry or whether I would be bullied. Perhaps you have similar childhood memories. Happily, many children feel free to express exactly who they are and how they feel. By the time I was a teenager, however, a radical change had taken place, and my mask was developing to filter emotions depending on the time and place.

I'd always felt more able to share emotions around feminine energy but, unfortunately for me, I had a household full of boys around me most of the time. We all competed for who could be the most masculine — and what we thought was masculine was to be rough and tough and show no fear. Heart and soul connections were replaced with physical and mental prowess. Those who were tough, sarcastic and had a carefree attitude towards authority were considered the leaders, while those who showed emotions and 'goody two-shoes' attitudes were quickly discarded as being sissies. Those behaviours became so ingrained that they defined who I became for many years.

I've also realised another wider problem we face is that even if we want to open up, we haven't been given the tools to do so. The traditional education system is still too focused and scored on academic and physical ability — though I would argue that, throughout my life, it's been my emotions that have had more control over my day-to-day decision making than anything I was ever taught at school. Some might argue that it's not the responsibility of the school system to teach us how to build emotional openness and resilience. Instead, this should be the responsibility of the family and the household. It's like we are all just trying to cope in this crazy world, pretending that our emotions should take a back seat to everything else.

No wonder so many of us feel so lonely, divorce is so high, and suicide is the biggest killer in Australia of males aged between 15 and 44. We've either forgotten as a society how to be open and connect, or we've just never had the tools do so — and so we just try to get on with it. Personally, I don't like the way that we just 'get on with it' and I certainly didn't like the way I just got on with it, choosing to dismiss something or someone rather than having the ability to be open and connect. I lost many wonderful relationships in my past because of my inability to want to care and be cared for, and I have seen far too many people around me take their own lives because of the same reason.

Just like in any other aspect of life when you're hoping to build something, you need the right tools before you can start connecting. Without these tools, you can feel like you're constantly fumbling and, unfortunately, if it becomes too hard, you may give up.

I have a wonderful picture that my dad painted of a green turtle. I wanted to hang it up in my hallway at home as a constant reminder for myself to 'be the turtle', a motto of mine that reminds me to slow down and go with the flow. I went to the shed, grabbed a nail and, for the life of me, I couldn't find my hammer. That picture stayed on my hallway floor collecting dust for quite some time because I didn't have the right tool for the job at hand. Being able to open up and connect to others is no different — we sometimes need the right tools.

When we created the Play for Your Life cards, I realised we had found the right tools for the job. We'd created something that was simple and effective, and that allowed people to take off their mask. They were simply talking to a pack of cards, and this didn't seem as vulnerable as talking to a person. I've played these cards all over the world, in many cultures and with all types of personalities, from one on one to a room of hundreds of people all partnering up and talking until the cows come home. I still am astounded by the depth of connection and openness that is created.

Playing the cards

So, now it's your turn to play a card game. On the following page the figure shows the eight cards (aligned with the eight wellness areas from part II) that, together, create health, happiness, balance and your overall wellbeing. Again, these areas really decide your ups and downs. At any time, your life can be good, bad, ugly, busy, quiet and lonely — and all the 'white noise' in your head can stop you being able to decipher what you might need to improve certain aspects. It's very hard to manage what you don't measure, and not fully comprehending how you got somewhere can stop you being able to move on. This is where the cards come in. Shall we start?

From the eight cards, choose a card that represents an area of your life that you're feeling good about at the moment (or perhaps just be a little better about than the others).

Now, ask yourself why you chose that card. Instead of reading over that question, pause and reflect. Think about all the positives within that area of your life. Are the positives in that area of your life sustainable? Do you find maintaining that area easy and, if not, what could you do to improve it?

You don't have to stop at just one area. If you're feeling good about other areas in the present moment, pick them out and ask yourself the same questions. The more cards you have in the positive pile, and that are sustainable in your life, the more head-space you have to look after the improvement cards.

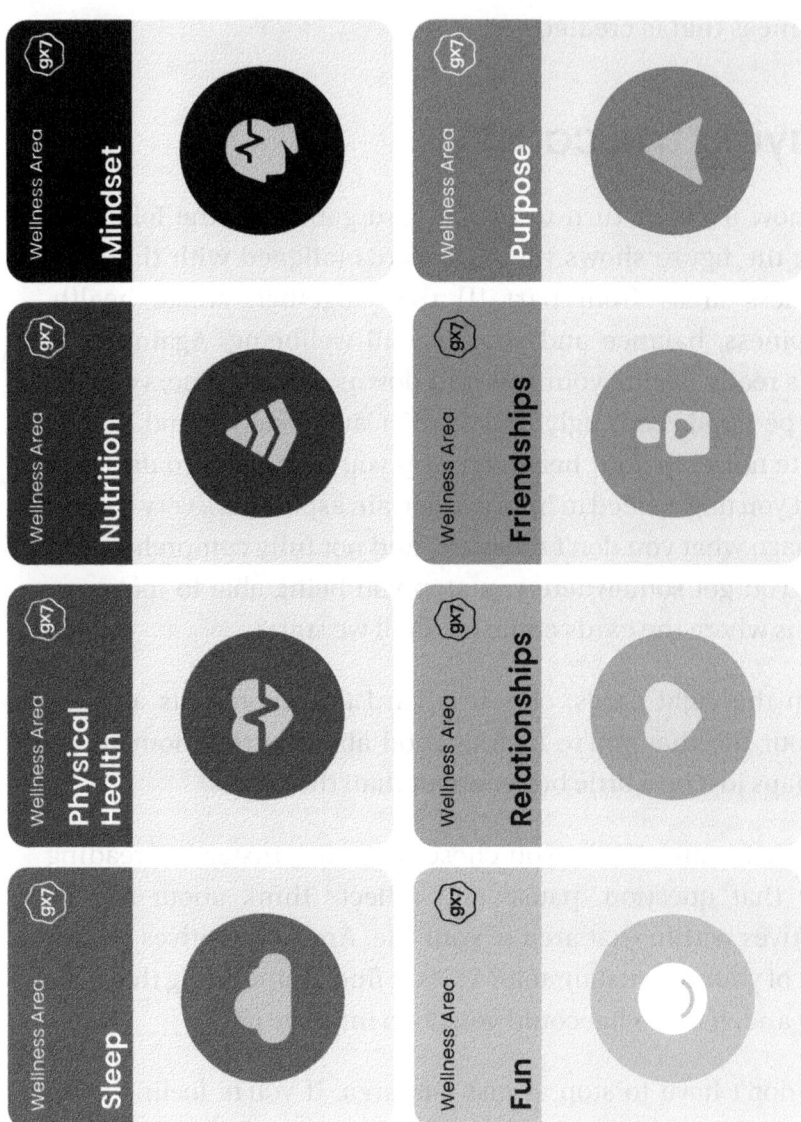

The GreenX7 Play for Your Life cards

If you're playing these cards with someone else, sit in the gratitude space with them, so they can see that life isn't all bad and they are achieving good things in certain areas of their lives.

Now look back at the cards and choose one that represents an area you would like to improve on — even if it's just for this week or month. Complete the following questions.

Why did you choose that card?

I really want you to stop here and create the time to reflect on this question. You will almost always know the answer, and just need to give it time to come to the surface.

_____

_____

_____

What do you feel you could do to improve this area?

Most, if not all, of the time you will have a solution. Write it down.

_____

_____

_____

When could you start to do this?

This to me is the most important piece, because what I've realised is that information is useless unless implemented. Write down a specific day or time for taking action.

_____

_____

_____

How did you go?

The cards have been developed and perfected over the years, but I've found that these three simple questions can help create a positive change in your wellbeing:

- What was the reason you chose that card?
- What do you feel you could do to improve it?
- When could you start to do this?

I've also found that most people know what they need to do — the card game simply allows them the time and space to talk openly about this. Once again, this highlights the importance of connection.

You can use these cards with your team and others you lead, to help guide them to their own discoveries and improvements. Note that I've put in place two conditions when playing the cards with someone else:

1. You must be 100 per cent present — no technology, no distractions. You are there to ask those three questions and to actively listen.

2. That person should be empowered to find their own solutions. You may know (or think you know) exactly what they need to do, but your role is to gently guide them to find their own solution, so they can own it. This will give them a greater chance of implementing it for change.

One of my favourite things is going to the post office with several packs of cards and addresses, knowing that someone, somewhere, is about to be healed by creating deeper connections.

CASE STUDY: A SOLIDER OPENS UP

I've run workshops for the Australian Defence Forces at their Soldier Recovery Centre, part of the Gallipoli Barracks in Brisbane. I would also go there for a few hours in the afternoon every couple of months to help soldiers recover from mental, emotional or physical wounds, and help them get back on track by using the GreenX7 tools.

The best part of these sessions was watching soldiers play the Play for Your Life cards with each other and really open up about what was going on. I made a pact with the soldiers that if they played the cards with a fellow soldier and they felt that person needed the cards more than they did, they would hand them over to help them heal. When they did, they would email me their address so I could send them another pack of cards for free. One solider in particular really ran with this idea. I don't know exactly how many packs of cards I sent to him, but every time I did it would make my heart sing, knowing that he was healing fellow soldiers by creating deeper conversations.

Here's what he had to say after our first workshop:

Thank you, Tim, for the eye-opening workshop you recently conducted with the Soldiers Recovery Centre. The way you highlighted the positive effects nature and mindfulness have on your individual perspective of life was incredible to watch and greatly appreciated by all the members who were lucky enough to attend. We now have more effective tools in our kit to help combat mental health, through staying connected and practising gratefulness.

The Play for Your Life cards are extremely helpful and really help us understand and put into practice the tools provided a lot easier. They have already helped right many things in my own life and have even helped my best mate open up about his anxiety—which I had no idea even existed. I've noticed it's a lot easier for some people to be open when addressing the cards.

I completely agree with and see the positive effects movement, water and especially nature as a whole have had on my overall wellbeing. GreenX7 has truly changed my life by helping me to consciously take time out to work on personal relationships and commit more genuine time to myself.

Thanks again, Tim — you're a legend and I'm so stoked we all got to take part in this workshop. We look forward to seeing you again!!

Scan the QR code below to learn more about the Play for Your Life cards.

Chapter 21

How full is your battery?

By this stage of the book, you no doubt know that when I ask 'How's your battery?', I'm not talking about your phone battery but your internal battery—the one that keeps you waking up every morning, hopefully with energy, vitality, willingness and a why.

Like most of us, I make a deliberate effort before I go to bed each night to make sure all my devices are plugged in and charging, so when I wake up the next morning, they are at full capacity. I do this because I need all my devices, and especially my phone, to perform at their best. I don't want my phone to die on me before the day is done, because it's a tool I use personally and professionally to succeed. As I outline at the start of this book, what I've realised is that my phone is a direct resemblance to how I treat my own mind and body.

When my own internal battery starts to get low, I start closing out people around me. When I get really low, my light starts to dim and I become only a fraction of my best self, both personally and professionally. I had a breakthrough moment when I realised that, just like my phone, I needed a way to measure my own internal battery—something to indicate whether I was merely surviving, just functioning, or truly thriving. A well-known saying in business, often misattributed to management guru Peter Drucker, is, 'What gets measured gets managed'. The same principle applies to us. If we don't take the time to assess our energy, wellbeing and resilience, how can we expect to manage them effectively? Understanding where we stand isn't just about awareness—it's also about taking control and making the necessary adjustments to live at our best.

Linking awareness with action

When my personal battery is full, I'm thriving. I'm in a state of flow, I effortlessly achieve my goals and I'm much happier within myself and with those around me. Life seems much easier, and I have a feeling of 'I've got this'. But, most importantly, I can feel that when I'm thriving, I become an inspiration to others around me. This fits with my purpose to inspire others to thrive sustainably.

Think about a time when your personal battery was full and you were thriving. How did it feel? How did your day go? How productive were you? How inspired were you to get out of bed and go to work? How resilient did you feel to your day-to-day challenges? Perhaps it's been so long since you have been able to thrive that you've forgotten what it feels like. For some people, functioning is their norm and so they benchmark themselves off that.

On the flip side, when my own internal battery starts to get low, I feel tired and uninspired, and the littlest things can cause me aggravation. I become impatient, and I look for the negatives instead of finding the positives. Worst of all, I don't like who I am and, honestly, I'm sure I could say the same for the people around me who have to put up with my surly behaviour.

How about you? Can you think about a time when your battery was low? Maybe you were tired, sick, stressed, anxious, waking up without purpose or feeling isolated from others. How did it feel? How did your day go? How productive were you? How inspired were you to get out of bed and go to work? How resilient did you feel when faced with your day-to-day challenges?

I remember very clearly a few years back when I realised how important recharging my battery was. It was a beautiful summer's day; January school holidays and our company Watersports Guru was in full swing. On this day, I was in my home office, grinding away like I had been for the past few months. GreenX7 had been given a wonderful opportunity to work with an international luxury hotel group and integrate our wellness program for their staff and guests. I had told myself that, just for the next few months, I'd throw caution to the wind, throw my daily rhythm (refer to chapter 19) out the window and go full pace while I built out the program and the technology that complemented it. Basically, I stopped taking my own advice. Little by little, my battery began to recede.

Over those few months, I stopped connecting to the GreenX7 tools and my battery charge was receding, I could feel myself going from thriving to functioning. Impatience and abruptness started creeping into my interactions with those around me. The worst of it was I stopped having fun — the thing I have built my life around. I know how important fun is for my mental health and that, without it, I start resenting those around me who are having fun. I was regressing into the very person I had spent so many years trying to move away from.

Which brings me back to a beautiful summer's day at Cudgen Creek, Kingscliff. I needed a break from the office, so I decided to head down to Watersports Guru and check in with how the staff were going. I jumped in the car and drove a few minutes from my home office to the creek. As I pulled into the carpark, the place was packed with people and I could see everyone out on the water having an awesome time. The water was crystal clear, and people were paddling, swimming, laughing and living their best lives. Typically, this makes my heart sing and brings a huge smile to my face because it's exactly why I created Watersports Guru — to help others reconnect with nature through fun experiences. Today, though, was a different story. My battery was low, I hadn't had any fun for months and I was looking for an excuse to vent my frustrations.

As I approached the tent where people were signing in and being briefed, instead of focusing on all the smiles and laughter, I focused on all the things that needed improving — life jackets not done up, paddles not in order, silly things that made no difference to people's happiness. I went up to my manager, Matt, pulled him aside and started to berate him for not running the place as it should be. He let me go on for about 30 seconds and then stopped me with the following: 'Tim, before you came, everyone here was having an awesome time. The energy was good and people were having fun. Instead of focusing on the good, you've brought in your negative energy and you're ruining everyone's mood. I think you should leave'.

What a slap in the face — being told by my manager to leave my own company, the one that I had started from nothing. I went to open my mouth to give him the boss speech — but then realised he was 100 per cent right. I was being an absolute idiot.

I apologised, turned away and walked back to my car with my tail between my legs, absolutely hating myself. Who had I become?!

It was in that moment that I vowed never to give up my rhythm, no matter how busy, successful or crazy things got. I realised that if I wanted to inspire people to become the best version of themselves, I needed to do the same. I also realised how important the framework we created at GreenX7 was in helping people to thrive sustainably — and how easy it was to slip back into unhealthy habits when the GreenX7 tools were ignored. Now, no matter what I'm doing and no matter where I am, I make sure I reconnect to recharge my battery each day.

In this modern world, we all have so many competing demands and life is so busy that many of us push ourselves through our day and collapse into bed at night exhausted. We have so many responsibilities as we try to balance work, kids and partners that just thinking about ourselves can be a chore. We've become so good at creating a life that we have to support that we've forgotten that we need to create a life that supports us! I still have to constantly remind myself to live within my means, so I have the time to look after my mental, emotional and physical self.

Yes, we are busy; however, when you say you're too busy for self-care, what you're probably really saying is that you're not prioritising your time to look after yourself, first and foremost.

Remember the battery zones I outlined in chapter 2. Are you surviving right now (battery between 0 and 50 per cent)? Are you functioning (between 50 and 70 per cent)? Maybe you are even thriving (80 per cent and above). If you are — well done! But if you have completely forgotten that life should be enjoyed, spent with friends and family frolicking and pondering, then it may be time to stop and reflect, and find a way to come back to your true north.

Checking your battery

Every time you look at your phone battery, I want you to think about your own battery and how you can make time today to recharge. To help with this, how would you like a quick tool to measure your own battery to understand where you are at this moment?

Now, I don't like to toot my horn often — growing up with so many brothers, the moment I did, I'd get whacked down fast — but I am very proud of what we were able to create. Through the GreenX7 app, we created a tool that:

- measures your wellbeing within 60 seconds

- tailors activities and suggestions based on what you need

- creates a language to share your wellbeing with others — as you ask each other, 'How's your battery?'

- empowers you to recharge your battery

- enables you to share with others so you've got the support you need.

The last point in the preceding list was, for me, the most important. Through knowing your battery charge, you're also given a way to share how you're going without putting up a wall or shutting down — especially important for us men who struggle with communicating our deeper emotions. I only wish I had this app when Mal was still around.

Now, it's your turn. Scan the provided QR code. You'll be prompted to answer eight questions on how you are feeling in the eight wellness areas (from part II) at the moment. Reflect on each one and answer honestly.

Once you have your results and can see which activities or suggestions will help recharge your battery, take one minute to map out the what, when, where and who. Skip back to the relevant chapter for each wellness area for more tips and action points. Either add the activity to your calendar or simply take action — no overthinking, just do it.

Next, think about someone who can be part of this journey with you. Who's the person you can share your battery charge with and vice versa, as you hold each other accountable? Who on your team might also benefit from being on this journey? Invite them through the app now.

For me, my crew includes my wife, my brother, and two close mates who keep tabs on me. Recently, I hit a rough patch — I was sick, exhausted and injured, thanks to a combination of a weird gut bacteria from travelling, sleepless nights with the kids and pushing too hard on an adventure. By the time I bounced back, my usual 85 per cent battery had dropped to 70 per cent. When I checked in, I saw I was low on fun, physical health and friendship.

Within five minutes of sharing my battery, my mate Ant had teed up a surf at Tugun (on the Gold Coast) for seven the next morning with the boys for a recharge. Just like that, I was back on track. That moment reinforced that what we've built works — it's not just a concept but also a way to live. It helps you create a lifestyle that allows you to get back on track to be the best version of yourself, and to support and be supported through the ups and downs of life.

CASE STUDY: A NOW THRIVING RELATIONSHIP BETWEEN TWO SISTERS

Carly and Ellen are sisters and both in their 20s. They grew up in a family with three children, but are five years apart and so were never particularly close. When Ellen left home, she spent a lot of time travelling overseas. When Ellen returned, she started feeling quite restless and flat, wondering what to do with her life now that she no longer had the excitement of travel.

After finding out Ellen was looking for something to improve her wellbeing and mental health, Carly introduced her to the GreenX7 app. They started sharing their wellness reports with each other through the connect feature and, over the next two years, their relationship transformed.

Carly says, 'We were never really close. When we used to see each other, we would ask "How are you?" and the answer would be "Good" or "Fine". Now, we have a much deeper connection with each other. Our relationship is now thriving, and a real friendship has blossomed'.

The app has become part of Carly and Ellen's daily groove—they enter their ratings for each of the eight wellness areas each time they get a notification to do so. They then get in touch with each other to offer support as needed. Carly says, 'If Ellen's fun area is low, I might text her and say, "Why don't we go for a beach walk?" One time I checked in with Ellen after I saw that her friendship area was low. It turned out she had been having some tough times with a close friend and it really helped her to talk to me about it. She actually said "I love you" after the conversation, which is the first time I remember her saying that to me.'

Ellen says that she likes how the app gives you a non-confronting way to admit where you might need some extra support. She says, 'Instead of having to ring Carly to say, "I'm not doing well", Carly can just see it from my battery report, and it sparks a conversation. It has really helped me to manage my stress better.'

Carly and Ellen like having a common language to use with each other — asking each other 'How's your battery?' has become part of their shared vocabulary. It has become an effortless way to check in on a deeper level with each other.

CONCLUSION

We've certainly covered a lot together in this book—including what wellbeing actually is, how to measure and share it with others and, most importantly, how to adopt a framework to guide you to thrive sustainably.

To recap:

- You've got your *purpose*, the reason you want to be the best version of yourself.

- You have created a rhythm around your *sleep*, and have a set time to go to sleep and wake up that will give you at least seven hours sleep.

- You are moving your body each day (preferably for 30 minutes at an elevated heart rate) to improve your *physical health*.

- You're looking after your *nutrition*, and eating the good stuff to feel good.

- You've created a growth *mindset* and are working on removing any limited beliefs you've formed to stop you from being your best self—such as 'I don't have time for this "being well" stuff!'

- You've included play in your life to boost your *fun*.
- You have made *friendships* more of a priority.
- The *relationships* you have with yourself and your loved ones have deepened.

And by bringing awareness to these areas of your life, you now know what is needed. You've made a deliberate effort to look after yourself, and can set an example for those around you, including your family and those you lead. Nice work!

I've also given you the 'secret sauce', the 'golden ticket', the 'winning formula', the stuff legends are made of, the one thing that is going to keep you on track for now and forever, a habit that is so powerful you wish you'd known about it years ago—your daily rhythm.

As I outline in chapter 19, your daily rhythm is the one non-negotiable you stick with each and every day—no ifs or buts about it. You build your life around this rhythm and your life will be better for it. As always, your focus should be building a life that supports you, and not one you're constantly having to support.

As a reminder, each day my target is to tick off all GreenX7 tools of movement, environment, earthing, time, connection, breath and reflection. (If it helps, think of this as creating a streak in your favourite app.)

Individually, all of these tools have their own benefits for your wellbeing. However, when they're combined together—boom! They create a sure-fire way to supercharge your battery and a valuable time saver.

As I outline in chapter 19, I want you to create your own rhythm, your own daily battery recharge, by combining as many GreenX7 tools as possible into one activity.

And I won't let you get away with any of the reasons why you can't and/or won't:

- 'I don't have time.'
- 'I'll start next week.'
- 'I already know this stuff.'
- 'I'm too tired to make changes.'
- 'I don't think it will work for me.'
- 'It's too much effort.'
- 'I don't want to give up the things I enjoy.'
- 'I don't have anyone to do it with.'
- 'I'll just push through.'
- 'I'm fine.'

You see, I used to ask Mal all the time how he was, and his response was always, 'I'm fine'. I believed him, and maybe he talked himself into believing it too — until he wasn't, and then he wasn't there. Making excuses won't recharge your battery, only actions will. Having all the information at your fingertips isn't enough; it's only the implementation of that knowledge that will move you forward in a positive direction.

Take the time now to write down three reasons why you need to make changes to your daily rhythm:

1. _____
2. _____
3. _____

With the information you now have, combined with your reasons why, you're ready to start creating new habits and a new improved version of you.

Start right now — write down an activity you can do today that combines as many GreenX7 tools as possible that's easily accessible, enjoyable and sustainable. As you develop your daily rhythm, I'll be right there with you, guiding you every step of the way through the chapters in this book, cheering you on from the sidelines because you've got this. You have the ability and willingness to wake up each morning with your reason why.

I'll leave you with a quote from Harvard business professor Karl Christensen, who argued that the measure of our lives is how well we help other people be better people. This idea guides my life each day, helping me to put my best foot forward, to make that deliberate effort and to ground myself to my reason why. Christensen argues,

> Don't worry about the level of individual prominence you have achieved; worry about the individuals you have helped become better people.[51]

You have the ability to help other people, including your loved ones and the people you lead, become better versions of themselves. But for this to happen, I believe you need to be better yourself.

I see you; I just hope that you see you too, and that from this day forward you will aspire to create a life that is worthy of you.

Keep charging, and I hope to see you soon.

THE GREENX7
MISSION

Our mission at GreenX7 is to measure and improve global wellbeing, one person at a time — starting with you. We want to create a 'prevention before prescription' lifestyle so we can reverse rates of loneliness, depression, chronic disease, dementia and other illnesses that stop us from being our healthiest, happiest selves. We do this through inspiring people to reconnect to themselves and others through nature.

What I've realised since starting this journey of mine in 2012 is that the more I recharge my battery, the better human I become. Most importantly, this makes me a *kinder* human being, and we need the world to be a kind place.

I hope that this book has been valuable for you and that, over the course of reading it, you have made incremental changes in your personal and professional life to reconnect and recharge. I hope that you, and others around you, are feeling the direct impact of this.

If you're a leader within your team, community or organisation (or even your country) I'd love you to help support our mission by being a role model and encouraging others to follow.

Leaders have an obligation and a responsibility to steer those who follow them in a positive direction. Whether you became a leader because you aspired to do so or through other circumstances, the decisions you make moving forward can have a profound impact on those around you. You can choose the mindset you wish to lead from, but remember — whichever way you go, it will have an impact.

I want to leave a legacy, a better world than the one I was born into. This may seem like a lofty goal, but I've already seen the impact that I'm making, purely because over a decade ago I chose to 'do better', both personally and professionally.

I invite you to do the same — creating meaningful, positive change in yourself and in those around you.

Keep charging!

Tim Jack Adams

JOIN THE GREENX7 COMMUNITY

Welcome to the GreenX7 community, where we inspire others to reconnect to themselves, each other and the natural environment for everyday wellness.

Now that you have the tools to reconnect and recharge your battery, you can start helping others to do the same. You now have the opportunity to help your loved ones and those you lead feel extraordinary, each and every day, no matter where you are.

Continue to recharge each day, and fill up your cup so you always have plenty to give others. This is your story, and every day you get to write a new page. It's time you become the author of a best seller!

If you want to join our community, jump on to our Instagram @ greenx7 and join us in our adventures in nature.

REFERENCES

1. See, for example, Breadon, P, Lachlan, F, Owain, E & Richardson, L (2023), *The Australian Centre for Disease Control* (ACDC)*: Highway to Health*, Grattan Institute.
2. Commonwealth of Australia (2022), *The National Obesity Strategy 2022–2032: At a Glance*, Health Ministers Meeting.
3. Hjelmborg, JvB, et al (2006), 'Genetic influence on human lifespan and longevity', *Human Genetics*, 119(3), 312–321.
4. Kerr, JA, et al (2025), 'Global, regional, and national prevalence of child and adolescent overweight and obesity, 1990–2021, with forecasts to 2050: A forecasting study for the Global Burden of Disease Study 2021', *The Lancet*, 405(10481), 785–812.
5. McCormak, P (2024), 'National Report Card: A concerning picture of the state of mental health and wellbeing in Australia', National Mental Health Commission.
6. Australian Bureau of Statistics (2023), 'Health conditions and risks', Australian Bureau of Statistics.
7. Black Dog Institute (2023), 'Facts & figures about mental health', Black Dog Institute.
8. Australian Bureau of Statistics (2023), 'Causes of Death, Australia' Australian Bureau of Statistics.

9. Bullen, J & Tarasov, A (2016), 'Australians spend eight times more hours per week looking at screens than with loved ones: survey', ABC News.

10. Rhodes, A (2017), 'Screen time and kids: What's happening in our homes?' Australian Child Health Poll, The Royal Children's Hospital Melbourne.

11. Australian Bureau of Statistics (2013), 'Australians spend one month a year sitting watching TV', Australian Bureau of Statistics.

12. Bullen, J & Tarasov, A (2016), 'Australians spend eight times more hours per week looking at screens than with loved ones: survey', ABC News.

13. Burrows, S (2017), 'Inmates spend more time outside than kids', Foundation for Economic Education.

14. Spinks collated these statistics based on data from the Australian Institute of Health and Wealth and the Australian Bureau of Statistics.

15. Huxtable, A (2024), 'Prescribing nature can improve happiness and reduce anxiety', *University of Sheffield News*; see also Carrington, D (2024), 'Better than medication: Prescribing nature works, project shows', *The Guardian*.

16. Texas Health Resources (2023), 'How much deep, light and REM sleep do you need?', Texas Health Resources.

17. See, for example, Suni, E (2023), 'How lack of sleep impacts cognitive performance and focus', Sleep Foundation; Goldstein, AN, & Walker, MP (2014), 'The role of sleep in emotional brain function', *Annual Review of Clinical Psychology*, 10(1), 679–708; and Willers, S (2025), 'The sleep-performance connection: Why rest is the key to better leadership', Workplace Wellbeing Professional.

18. Schnohr, P, et al (2018), 'Various leisure-time physical activities associated with widely divergent life expectancies: The Copenhagen City Heart Study', Mayo Clinic Proceedings, 93(12), pp. 1775–1785; Spring KE, Holmes ME, Smith JW

(2020), 'Long-term tennis participation and health outcomes: An investigation of 'lifetime' activities', *International Journal of Exercise Science*, 13(7), pp. 1251–1261.

19. See, for example, Paffenbarger, RS, et al (1986), 'Physical activity, all-cause mortality, and longevity of college alumni', *New England Journal of Medicine*, 314, pp. 605–613; McDowell-Larsenm S (2023), 'The good health and leadership connection', Center for Creative Leadership; Join The Collective (2023), 'Unveiling the power of physical fitness in enhancing leadership', Join The Collective; and Aaron (2024), 'Physical health and leadership performance', Leader Navigation.

20. LeWine, HE (reviewer) (2024), 'Understanding the stress response', Harvard Health Publishing, Harvard Medical School; Godman, H (2023), 'Hidden causes of weight gain', Harvard Health Publishing, Harvard Medical School.

21. Mayo Clinic Staff (2022), 'Exercise and stress: Get moving to manage stress', Mayo Clinic; Werner, C & Dias, A (2022), 'Emotional eating: What you should know', healthline; Volkow, ND, Wang, GJ, Tomasi, D & Baler, RD (2012), 'Obesity and addiction: Neurobiological overlaps', *Obesity Reviews*, 14(1).

22. Dunbar, R (2017), 'Breaking bread: The functions of social eating', *Adaptive Human Behavior and Physiology*, Vol 3, pp. 198–211; Novotney, A (2019), 'The risks of social isolation', American Psychological Association.

23. Black Dog Institute (2023), 'Facts & figures about mental health', Black Dog Institute.

24. For more in this area, see Brown, S & Vaughan, C (2010), *Play: How it Shapes the Brain, Opens the Imagination, and Invigorates the Soul*, Scribe Publications.

25. Raypole, C (2022), 'How to hack your hormones for a better mood', healthline.

26. Csikszentmihalyi, M (1990), *Flow: The psychology of optimal experience*. Harper & Row.

27. Csikszentmihalyi, M (1990), *Flow: The psychology of optimal experience*. Harper & Row; Bartholomeyczik K, Knierim MT, Weinhardt C (2023), 'Fostering flow experiences at work: A framework and research agenda for developing flow interventions', *Frontiers in Psychology*, Jul 7;14:1143654.

28. Casey, S, Stevens, L, Dempster, A & Hewish, A (2022), *Connections Matter: A report on the impacts of loneliness in Australia*, Groundswell Foundation and KPMG.

29. To take a deep dive into this area, check out any of the following: Cacioppo, JT & Patrick, W (2008), *Loneliness: Human nature and the need for social connection*, Norton & Company; Holt-Lunstad, J. (2022), 'Social connection as a public health issue: The evidence and a systemic framework for prioritizing the "social" in social determinants of health', *Annual Review of Public Health*, vol 43; Murthy, V (2023), *Together: The healing power of human connection in a sometimes lonely world*, Profile Books; Putnam, RD (2000), *Bowling Alone: The collapse and revival of American community*, Simon & Schuster; Turkle, S (2015), *Reclaiming Conversation: The power of talk in a digital age*, Penguin Press; and Wilson, RS, et al (2007), 'Loneliness and risk of Alzheimer disease', *Archives of General Psychiatry*, 64(2), 234–240.

30. Holt-Lunstad, J, Smith, TB, Baker, M, Harris, T & Stephenson, D (2015), 'Loneliness and social isolation as risk factors for mortality: A meta-analytic review', *Perspectives on Psychological Science*, 10(2), 227–237.

31. For more information, see Chapman, G (1992), *The Five Love Languages: How to express heartfelt commitment to your mate*, Northfield Publishing. This one was an eye-opener for me!

32. Godman, H (2014), 'Regular exercise changes the brain to improve memory, thinking skills', Harvard Health Publishing, Harvard Medical School.

33. Teri, L, Logsdon, RG & McCurry, SM (2008), 'Exercise interventions for dementia and cognitive impairment: The Seattle Protocols', *Journal of Nutrition, Health and Aging*, 12(6):391–394.

34. Sleiman, SF, et al (2016), 'Exercise promotes the expression of brain derived neurotrophic factor (BDNF) through the action of the ketone body β-hydroxybutyrate', *eLife*, Jun 2;5:e15092.

35. To deep dive into the benefits of spending time in forests and other natural environments, check out the following: Li, Q (2009), 'Effect of forest bathing trips on human immune function', *Environmental Health and Preventive Medicine*, 15(1), pp. 9–17; Peterfalvi, A, et al (2021), 'Forest bathing always makes sense: Blood pressure-lowering and immune system-balancing effects in late spring and winter in central Europe', *International Journal of Environmental Research and Public Health*, 18(4):2067; Bratman, GN, et al (2019), 'Nature and mental health: An ecosystem service perspective', *Science Advances*, 5(7); Weir, K (2020), 'Nurtured by nature', *Monitor on Psychology*, 51(3); and Mental Health Foundation (2021), 'Nature: How connecting with nature benefits our mental health', *Mental Health Foundation*.

36. Pretty, J, Peacock, J, Sellens, M & Griffin, M (2005), 'The mental and physical health outcomes of green exercise', *International Journal of Environmental Health Research*, 15(5):319–37.

37. Thompson Coon, J, et al (2011), 'Does participating in physical activity in outdoor natural environments have a greater effect on physical and mental wellbeing than physical activity indoors? A systematic review', *Environmental Science and Technology Journal*, 1;45(5):1761–72.

38. For more information on the benefits of sunshine and vitamin D, see the following: Holick, MF (2008), 'Vitamin D and sunlight: Strategies for cancer prevention and other health benefits', *Clinical Journal of the American Society of Nephrology*, 3(5), pp. 1548–1554; Dresden, D (2020), 'What to know about the health benefits of sunlight', Medical News Today; Aranow, C (2011), 'Vitamin D and the immune system', *Journal of Investigative Medicine*, 59(6), pp. 881–886.

39. Howard, PJ (2006), *The Owner's Manual for the Brain: Everyday Applications from Mind-Brain Research*, 3rd ed, Bard Press.

40. For much more information on the benefits of earthing, see the following: Brown, R, Chevalier, G & Hill, M (2010), 'Pilot study on the effect of grounding on delayed-onset muscle soreness', *Journal of Alternative and Complementary Medicine*, 16(3):265–273; Chevalier, G, Sinatra, ST & Oschman, JL (2012), 'Earthing: Health implications of reconnecting the human body to the Earth's surface electrons', *Journal of Environmental and Public Health*, p. 291541; Chevalier, G, Mori, K, Oschman, JL, Kenner, T & Brown, R (2015), 'The effects of grounding (earthing) on inflammation, the immune response, wound healing, and prevention of chronic inflammation and autoimmune diseases', *Journal of Inflammation Research*, 8: 83–96; and Ghaly, M & Teplitz, D (2004), 'The biological effects of grounding the human body during sleep as measured by cortisol levels and subjective reporting of sleep, pain, and stress', *Journal of Alternative and Complementary Medicine*, 10(5): 767–776.

41. Ober, C, Sinatra, ST, & Zucker, M (2010), *Earthing: The *st Important Health Discovery Ever?*, Basic Health ions.

42. Weekly time allocations based on data from the Australian Bureau of Statistics, including Australian Bureau of Statistics (2022), 'How Australians use their time', Australian Bureau of Statistics; and Australian Bureau of Statistics (2022), 'Unpaid work and care: Census', Australian Bureau of Statistics.

43. Bullen, J & Tarasov, A (2016), 'Australians spend eight times more hours per week looking at screens than with loved ones: survey', ABCNews.

44. Mineo, L (2017), 'Harvard study, almost 80 years old, has proved that embracing community helps us live longer, and be happier', *The Harvard Gazette*, Harvard University.

45. Mineo, L (2017), 'Harvard study, almost 80 years old, has proved that embracing community helps us live longer, and be happier', *The Harvard Gazette*, Harvard University.

46. Vaillant, G (2013), 'What are the secrets to a happy life?' *Greater Good Magazine*.

47. Bullen, J & Tarasov, A (2016), 'Australians spend eight times more hours per week looking at screens than with loved ones: survey', ABCNews.

48. Russo, MA, Santarelli, DM & O'Rourke, D (2017), 'The physiological effects of slow breathing in the healthy human', *Breathe*; Blount, A (2021), 'Deep breathing helps ease anxiety', PsychCentral.

49. For more on the benefits of slow or careful breathing, see the following: Merschel, M (2023), 'It's not just inspiration — careful breathing can help your health', *American Heart Association News*; Blanchfield, T (2022), 'The benefits of deep breathing', *Verywell Mind*; and Bence, S (2024), '8 health benefits of deep breathing (diaphragmatic breathing)', *Verywell Health*.

50. Vaillant, G (2009), 'Yes, I stand by my words, "Happiness equals love—full stop"', *Positive Psychology News*.

51. Christensen, CM (2010), 'How will you measure your life?', *Harvard Business Review*.

Printed and bound by CPI Group (UK) Ltd, Croydon, CR0 4YY

05/08/2025

14714017-0001